RIDERS IN THE SKY

Other western books from Gibbs Smith, Publisher

COWBOY CURMUDGEON
And Other Poems
by Wallace McRae

COWBOY POETRY
A Gathering
Edited by Hal Cannon

COWBOY POETRY COOKBOOK
Menus and Verse for Western Celebrations
by Cyd McMullen and Anne Wallace McMullen

NEW COWBOY POETRY
A Contemporary Gathering
Edited by Hal Cannon

OLD-TIME COWBOY SONGS
Song book and tape
by the Bunkhouse Orchestra

RIDERS in the SKY

TOO SLIM

RANGER DOUG

WOODY PAUL

WITH TEXAS BIX BENDER

GIBBS·SMITH
P
PUBLISHER

PEREGRINE SMITH BOOKS

SALT LAKE CITY

First edition

95 94 93 92   10 9 8 7 6 5 4 3 2 1

**This is a Peregrine Smith Book, published by
Gibbs Smith, Publisher**
P.O. Box 667
Layton, UT 84041

Design and typography by J. Scott Knudsen
Linotronic output by Blake Typographers
Cartoon illustrations by Fisher Design
Front cover photograph , Señor McGuire, © 1991 Sony
Music Entertainment, Inc, Courtesy Sony Music
Entertainment, Inc.
Back cover photograph © 1991, Peter Nash

Manufactured in Singapore by Times Publishing Group

Library of Congress Cataloging-in-Publication Data

Riders in the Sky / Ranger Doug, Woody Paul & Too Slim, with
Texas Bix Bender.
          p. cm.
      ISBN 0-87905-462-X
      1. Riders in the Sky. 2. Musicians—United States—
      Biography.
ML421.R5R5 1992
781.642'982'2—dc20
  [B]   91-37387
                              CIP
                              MN

FOR ALL OUR KIDS,

LIZA, PAUL DAVID,

SALLY ANNE, JOE, FRANK,

LILY, ANNIE LAURIE,

REBECCA, JAMIE, JACOB,

CASEY, ALICE,

AND (PENDING) . . .

& SADDLE PAL SAL.

WHERE DO WE COME IN?

A Highly Subjective History of Riders In The Sky

by Ranger Doug

From our first publicity photo session. My, how serious. When we went to TV, CBS advised us to keep our guns in our holsters.

I RECALL A CHILL NOVEMBER EVENING IN 1977, when Patti Hall, a delightful, lovely, and talented California-transplanted folksinger called to ask me to fill in for her at Nashville's darkest, dankest folk club/songwriter's showcase. She pleaded illness; I pleaded insanity and said yes, though I knew the money would be minuscule. I'd been doing a solo singing-cowboy act for a while, but I longed to hear the harmony on those songs I heard in my head, and I asked two old pals, Fred LaBour (yes, he was just Fred then) and Bill Collins to put together a cowboy trio in a matter of a couple of days. The results were more ragged than you would suspect, but the seed had been planted: we laughed for days over what we'd done and said for those dozen or so people at Herr Harry's Phranks 'n' Steins, and we vowed to do it again soon.

By the first part of 1978 we were playing a night or two a week pretty steadily, learning new songs, bringing a live cactus, saddles, and tumbleweeds to the shows. I was quickly promoted to Ranger Doug, Fred became Too Slim, and Windy Bill now rounded out the stalwart trio which, after a desperate search for a name, Too Slim had christened Riders in the Sky, after seeing the title of a Sons of the Pioneers' reissue album.

Spring 1978, on our way to one of our very first dates.
Windy Bill Collins, Too Slim, Ranger Doug.

It was an exciting time for us: here was music that was challenging and fun to play. We developed a loose and loopy act in small clubs and quickly gained exposure, notoriety, even a tandem of managers as eager and inexperienced as we were. We scrambled for new repertoire, began to write our own songs in the tradition, juggled our "real" jobs with our blossoming cowboy career. By the fall of that year we had to make some hard choices. I left a secure job with great people at the Country Music Foundation, Slim left Dicky Lee's road band for a very uncertain future as singing cowboys—in an era which wanted none—and as cutups and comedians in a town filled with serious singer-songwriters. Windy Bill chose to stay with Dicky Lee, and we replaced him with a guitarist, singer, and songwriter named Tumbleweed Tommy Goldsmith, whose cerebral humor replaced Windy Bill's more manic style.

I think it was at a listening room called the Old Time Pickin' Parlor that an apparition appeared to us one evening, a slow-drawling mountain man with a fiddle, who said with characteristic tact and modesty: "You boys really need me to help you out." After a lot of debate, old-time fiddle champ, M.I.T. PhD, born-again writer of cowboy songs Woody Chrisman joined the trail drive and immediately became Woody Paul, and we began several rough and wild and wonderful years as Riders In The Sky, hanging on by the skin of our teeth while we tried to paste together an impossible career.

Yes, this is Sheriff John. No western book would be complete without him. He was one of our childhood heroes.

Winters were the worst (Tumbleweed Tommy quit that first winter, and after a couple of brief replacement attempts we remained a trio for a decade before Joey the Cowpolka King accompanied us on accordion for a year and a half in 1989–1990; he's still a big part of "Riders Radio Theater," our recordings, the occasional live show, and our TV show). Several winters Woody fixed Volkswagens, Slim did puppets at the public library and galvanized metal, I did freelance writing and cut and sold firewood, not to mention those Sunday nights playing banjo at Shakey's.

But somehow, something good always happened, or was about to happen, and we never lost heart . . . for long, anyway. We made our first album (*Three On The Trail*) for Rounder in 1979–1980; we were frequent guests on the "Grand Ole Opry," we appeared on "Austin City Limits" in 1981, we were made members of the Opry cast June 19, 1982, we kept recording an album a year for Rounder, the road dates got a little better and a little better and a little better yet; we got a show called "Tumbleweed Theater" that appeared on a brand new cable network,

The Nashville Network, in March of 1983. We grew up some as individuals, and then some more; we continued to write and develop our skits and songs and characters, always pursuing a distinct individuality within a traditional style, bringing our individual talents to the tradition as well as the influences of the styles we'd played and studied and been influenced by, ranging far from pure western music: bebop, bluegrass, big band, rock and roll, Dixieland, Hawaiian, folk, country, mariachi, etc., etc., etc.

Somewhere along the line we crossed the barrier between a struggling band and a real career. It wasn't so much the money, the ability to actually be making a decent, if unspectacular, living at it (though people sometimes still ask after a show what we do for a living during the week—even on a Tuesday night in Oregon!); no, it was just that this is how we were becoming known, this was a national act, it was, it was . . . a career.

Milestones seem, in retrospect, to flash by along memory trail: the 500th appearance, the 40th state played (we're up to 46 now), the first, and second, and third overseas tours, the 1,000th appearance, and the 1,500th and 2,000th (we're fast approaching 2,500 as I write), national TV appearances, more Rounder albums (7 in all), another "Austin City Limits," a major label at last (MCA, for four albums), awards for albums and songs, a Christmas special on the Nashville Network, "Riders Radio Theater" being born and dying on WPLN in Nashville, rising again, like Lazarus, in Cincinnati over WVXU. And just within the last year or so the move to Columbia Records, and, of course, the TV show, the next step, the huge uncertainty and adventure that awaits us as we put this book, and this chapter of our career, to bed.

Who could have dreamed it? No one could have planned it. It has been a miracle and an adventure all the way, constantly creative, changing, challenging . . . which is why, though we've suffered exhaustion a time or two, we have yet to suffer burnout. After 14 years we are still creating, still as excited as we were the first time we performed *Blue Montana Skies* or *Blue Bonnet Lady,* still as in love with the West and its music as the day we first tried to sing it.

We still love bringing the West to the people of this country, and others, making audiences misty-eyed one moment, roll with laughter the next, smile in appreciation the next. You couldn't plan a career like this, but we're sure glad it happened. All along, it's been The Cowboy Way.

Performing on "Austin City Limits," 1981. Too Slim had hair, Woody Paul had long hair, and Ranger Doug has 40 extra pounds.

June 19, 1982, the night we became members of the Grand Ole Opry. A jubilant Too Slim, a blissful Ranger Doug, an alert and aware Woody Paul, Opry manager Hal Durham, and the late, great Ernest Tubb, who first introduced us.

Early years. The fourth man is Tumbleweed Tommy Goldsmith.

9

THE COWBOY WAY

It's the courage of the pioneers who crossed a continent's span
It's the spirit of the red men who shed their blood to save their land
It's the will to know the truth, good or bad, come what may
It's a heart that's free and grateful, it's the cowboy way
It's the strength to say you're sorry, admit that you were wrong
It's the wisdom, too, to recognize the time you must be strong
It's a love of Nature's creatures in their struggle and their play
It's the quiet flame of justice, it's the cowboy way
It's the hand to help a neighbor or a stranger in their need
It's the love of humankind with not a thought of race or creed
It's the courage of convictions, without posture or display
It's the peaceful sleep of children, it's the cowboy way
It's the moment that you take before the words you might regret
It's the time you give to others with no thought of what you'll get
It's the time you take in smelling all the roses on the way
It's doing just the best you can, it's the cowboy way

RANGER DOUG
Idol of American Youth

WESTERN MUSIC: WHAT IT IS

THERE ARE A LOT OF BUCKAROOS AND BUCKARETTES out there
who know exactly where our musical roots flourish, and
others who assume that, musically, we come from the
planet Debbie. Some of our fans know every record
Gene, Roy, Tex and the Pioneers ever made; yet there's
a whole generation out there who—much to our aston-
ishment—never heard of our heroes. So it seemed like
a Rangerly idea to take a few pages to sketch, in words
and photographs, a brief history of singing cowboys,
western music, and where we fit in this musical style
and tradition.

The cowboys of yesteryear sang at work, of course,
probably not any more or less than they do today, which,
if you think about it, is really not all that much. There
was, for some, a bit of music in the evening—some songs or
poetry—but the romantic image of cowboy singers is an out-
growth of America's endless fascination with the American
West, explored and exploited as drama and romance as early as the
Buffalo Bill Wild West Shows and the Ned Buntline dime novels of a
hundred years ago—a wild and woolly west being mythologized as it was
still a living thing!

This translated easily to film as that medium swept the nation in the early
part of this century—and radio as well when that became popular in the 1920s,
and on thick 78rpm records at about the same time—and when sound came to
films in the late 1920s, what was more natural than adding music to the stirring
western sagas already flickering on screens all across America and the world. The
first cowboy star to sing on screen was enormously successful silent-film star Ken
Maynard, who sang "My Tonia" in *In Old Arizona* in 1929.

Dick Foran serenades
his horse.

Bob Nolan, composer of "Tumbling Tumbleweeds" and "Cool Water," among many others.

The cowboy songs of the previous decades—some folk, some adapted from poetry published in stockmen's journals, some written by gifted amateurs and semi-professionals—were quickly used up in early films. I'm thinking here of longish songs of cowboys at work and at play, of farfetched tall tales, of sentimental tales of homesickness, and tragedy: "Tying Knots in the Devil's Tail," "The Strawberry Roan," "The Zebra Dun," "Little

Andy Parker (center) and the Plainsmen, late 1940s.

The Sons of the Pioneers, early 1940s: Pat Brady, Hugh Farr, Lloyd Perryman, Roy Rogers, Bob Nolan, Karl Farr, Tim Spencer.

Joe the Wrangler," "When the Work's All Done This Fall," and the like.

There quickly became a demand and a need for new songs and, given Ken Maynard's limited vocal appeal, new singers as well. Enter radio star and former Jimmie Rodgers sound-alike Gene Autry, who debuted in a Maynard film (*In Old Santa Fe*, 1934), went on to make a serial (*Phantom Empire*), and then began starring in a series of westerns, beginning with *The Last Roundup* and *Tumbling Tumbleweeds* and ending with *Last of the Pony Riders* in 1953. His sincere, pleasant demeanor and friendly, avuncular voice made him an overnight star, but the titles of those first two starring films have a tale to tell as well: they were both nationally popular cowboy songs written by a new breed of songwriter (Billy Hill and Bob Nolan respectively)—men who had a gift for folklike melodies that lent themselves to airy harmony, and a gift for lyrics that were sweeping, emotional, visionary, and lyrically poetic, very different from any popular or country music of the day.

Hill composed a number of similar songs: *Empty Saddles, The Old Spinning Wheel,* and *Call of the Canyon,* among others. Young Len Slye brought Nolan and another extremely gifted songwriter, Tim Spencer, together to form the Pioneer Trio in 1933; they became the Sons of the Pioneers with the addition of classic members Hugh and Karl Farr (fiddle and guitar), lyric tenor Lloyd Perryman, and Pat Brady, who somewhat ironically replaced Slye in 1937, when Len left the group to break into films on his own, first as Dick Weston, then as Roy Rogers.

These Pioneers defined the western style in which we sing, the tradition in which we follow: graceful harmony, soaring yet masculine, swinging a little but not dance oriented, lyrically poetic, no longer confined to the work, play, braggadocio or tragedy of the working cowboy but a celebration of the West itself—its fierce beauty, its matchless vistas, its variety, loneliness, grandeur, its seemingly endless possibilities for freedom.

Bob Nolan and Tim Spencer wrote hundreds of such stirring songs for films, radio, and record, and they form the core of every cowboy trio's repertoire: *Tumbling Tumbleweeds, Cool Water, Skyball Paint, Blue Prairie, Everlasting Hills of Oklahoma, Timber Trail,* and on and on and on and on and on. Other groups quickly followed

Above: The Jimmy Wakely Trio, c. 1940: Johnny Bond, Jimmy Wakely, Dick Rhinehart. Below: Foy Willing and the Riders of the Purple Sage, late 1940s: (left-right, top) Al Sloey, Bud Sievert, Scotty Harrell, (bottom) Jerry Vaughn, Foy Willing, Johnny Paul.

13

their lead: Stuart Hamblen and his Lucky Stars, Foy Willing and the Riders of the Purple Sage, the Jimmy Wakely Trio, Andy Parker and the Plainsmen, The Cass County Boys, and many others who brought great songs and great harmony to the style.

Likewise, singing cowboys by the scores followed the trails Ken Maynard and Gene Autry blazed, as every major and minor studio wanted their own: Tex Ritter, Ray Whitley, Dick Foran, Fred Scott, Smith Ballew, Bob Baker, Bill Boyd and many others (including Dorothy Page, a singing cowgirl, and Herb Jeffries, a Black singing cowboy) in the 1930s, and Eddie Dean, Jimmy Wakely, Monte Hale, Ken Curtis, and Rex Allen in the 1940s. There were a zillion cameo and singin' sidekick roles for popular cowboy entertainers as well: Bob Wills, Spade Cooley, Elton Britt, Red Foley, and Ernest Tubb, among many others. Each of these singing cowboys was special and unique; what's important here (as opposed to a detailed history) is not who they were, but *that* they were: never had the cowboy and the West been so celebrated in music for a period of two decades, and the songs of that twenty-year span remain our inspiration, our foundation, our *raison d'être*.

By 1955 this glorious era was just about over. Too Slim thinks it's because the hats got smaller (check it out, it's true!), but whatever the reason, the innocent, playful, optimistic westerns of the 1930s, with their rollicking trail songs and poetic looks at nature were a far cry from the violent, surly, ill-tempered psychological westerns of the 1950s, and by the 1960s western films were rare except for series television, and even there Gene Autry's and Roy Rogers' once-popular TV shows were long off the air.

On record, Tex and Rex and Roy were still making occasionally popular records, mostly in the country field, while musical polymath Marty Robbins kept the tradition alive—albeit largely in outlaw guise—as a part of his incredibly versatile career. The Pioneers never stopped touring and recording—indeed they are still going strong today—but the movement as a whole gradually slipped from public consciousness. It ceased to be vital and creative (for the most part; there were, of

course, exceptions); it became the stuff of nostalgia for the faithful, doubly evocative of bygone eras—one the Old West which it celebrated, the other its own golden age: glory the 1930s and 1940s.

In a sense it was forgotten but not gone: groups who sang for tourists at chuck wagons in scenic parts of the West (Colorado Springs, Jackson Hole, Estes Park, Durango) kept the sound and style alive. Roy and the Pioneers popped up on TV in everything from "Hee Haw" to the "Muppet Show." It surfaced in the 1970s music, fueled only a little by nostalgia, but more by a generation of music appreciators raised on acoustic music, who looked for an integrity they found in folk music, something at the same time nostalgic, campy, yet genuinely moving. In retrospect, the time was right for someone to revive this style in the '70s, but as for our part, I can tell you we sure didn't have the benefit of that hindsight. We just wanted to sing those beautiful old songs because the harmony was unique and beautiful and complex, and so were the lyrics. We wanted to perform and write similar songs which celebrated nature and the earth and the West, the opposite of the "outlaw" movement then all the rage in country music. The time was indeed right for what we had to offer, though we didn't consciously know it; we took what we could, created what we could, and basically just got on and rode with it. It took off like a bronc out of the chutes, and despite a few hard times, we've never looked back.

This, then, is where we come from, musically. If you love the West and its music at all, I'd advise buying reissued records by any or all of these artists—they *can* be found, with enough work, and it's work well worth it. There are a number of current artists who likewise are making great western music, including the Reinsmen, the Sons of the San Joaqin, Robert Wagoner, soloists like Don Edwards and Gary McMahan. The Sons of the Pioneers are still recording, and the remarkable Michael Martin Murphey is revitalizing western music in the country music mainstream. It's a long, historic, and rich tradition, but it is also very much a living, vital tradition. We are proud to be a part of it.

Gene Autry

14

Tex Ritter (right), late 1930s.

Fred Scott

DEADWOOD DARLENE'S
THE BEST IN PRAIRIE LUBRICANTS!

$9.99 CATALOG OF VALUES!

If you're one of the millions of Americans who love to find those slick, trendy mail order catalogs in your mailbox, then hold onto your hats buckaroos and buckarettes, 'cause here comes the most amazing compendium of unbelievable merchandise ever offered to the American public!

EVERY ITEM IN THIS CATALOG IS AVAILABLE ONLY FROM DEADWOOD DARLENE'S AND EVERY ITEM IN THIS CATALOG IS **PRICED AT ONLY $9.99!!!**

Saddle Whiz (Cheese Flavored) 55 Gallon Drum
"No more sticky saddle"

WE HAVE THE SOLUTIONS FOR ALL YOUR HOME-ON-THE-RANGE PROBLEMS!

For example: What do you do if your herd sulks up and becomes cantankerous over little things, like branding, that never seemed to bother them before? Get out your Sharper Image and order a Swiss paring knife?

No! You get out your Deadwood Darlene $9.99 catalog of values and order a gross of "udder-butter on a rope!"

"Polled Hereford Horn Polish"

Udder-Butter on a Rope For Contented Cows!

"Before I discovered udder-butter on a rope my herd was the surliest in the state. Now they're docile, cud-chewing sweetie-pies! Thank you, Deadwood Darlene!

Sincerely,
Madonna

HERE ARE MORE STARTLING TESTIMONIALS!

"Your bio-feedbag has worked wonders with my jackass. Before I bought him one he was the surliest critter on the face of this planet. But not any more! Thanks to you, Deadwood Darlene, he's the mellowest jackass in the world! Of course, he's still a jackass.

Sincerely,
Barbara Bush

Cow nose mood ring
(it changes colors to indicate your cow's mood)

The Bio-Feedbag

Just attach the two color-coded wires to the earphones, put them over his ears, adjust the monitor, slip the feedbag on and in no time you'll have a centered, calm critter ready for a productive, giving day on the prairie.

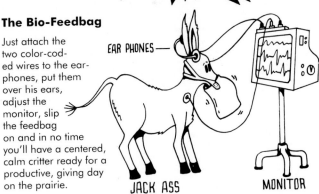

EAR PHONES —

JACK ASS   MONITOR

THE BIO-FEED BAG

Deadwood Darlene's prairie lubricants are the official lubricants of the Dallas Cheerleaders.

"I couldn't rope a fence post until I found out about Deadwood Darlene's "rope wax with organic stiffeners." Now I'm nailing everything that moves! Thanks, Deadwood Darlene!

Sincerely,
Donald Trump

Rope Wax With Organic Stiffeners

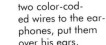

Krazy Kow Kompound
Spruce up those dinged-up dogies

To order, simply pick up the phone and dial 1-900-DARLENE!

Your catalog will be hand delivered to your door by a uniformed agent of the United States Government.

SPECIAL NOTE: If you order today we'll also send you, absolutely free, an additional scintillating and provocative catalog from the famed **FREDERICK'S OF DEADWOOD.**

Yes the romance of the range, Frederick's style!

Featuring "The Peek-A-Boo Bucking Cinch—it rounds 'em up and heads 'em out!"

"See-through saddle blankets!"

And the scentsational new scent of the bunkhouse "eau-dee-lay-de-oh!"

Nowhere else will you find these items!

Eau-dee-lay-de-oh!

FAMOUS CHARACTERS

TOO JAWS

In his hay-day he was at least the fourth or fifth smartest horse in the movies. Lately, as you can see by his picture, he's really let himself go. But after a long drying-out period at the Death Valley Rehab Center he's on the comeback trail and making numerous personal appearances with Riders In The Sky.

"It's tough to come back and die again." (After appearing with the Riders at a show at The Days End in Tahoe.)

"I spoke with Francis, The Talking Mule the other day . . . what a jackass."

"Aah Aah Aaaah."

Too Jaws, dying again. (Photo © 1986 Alan L. Mayor)

High Sheriff Drywall. (Photo © 1989 Don Putnam)

HIGH SHERIFF DRYWALL

One of the great boggled minds of the twentieth century. When not displaying immense ineptitude enforcing the laws of Tumbleweed County, the High Sheriff is a stupefying Elvis impersonator recording hits like "Living In A Mobile Home" and "Remodeled Home, Remodeled Heart" on the Skilsaw label.

FAMOUS DRYWALL QUOTES:

"Sir?"

"The What?"

"I don't get it and I don't think about it either."

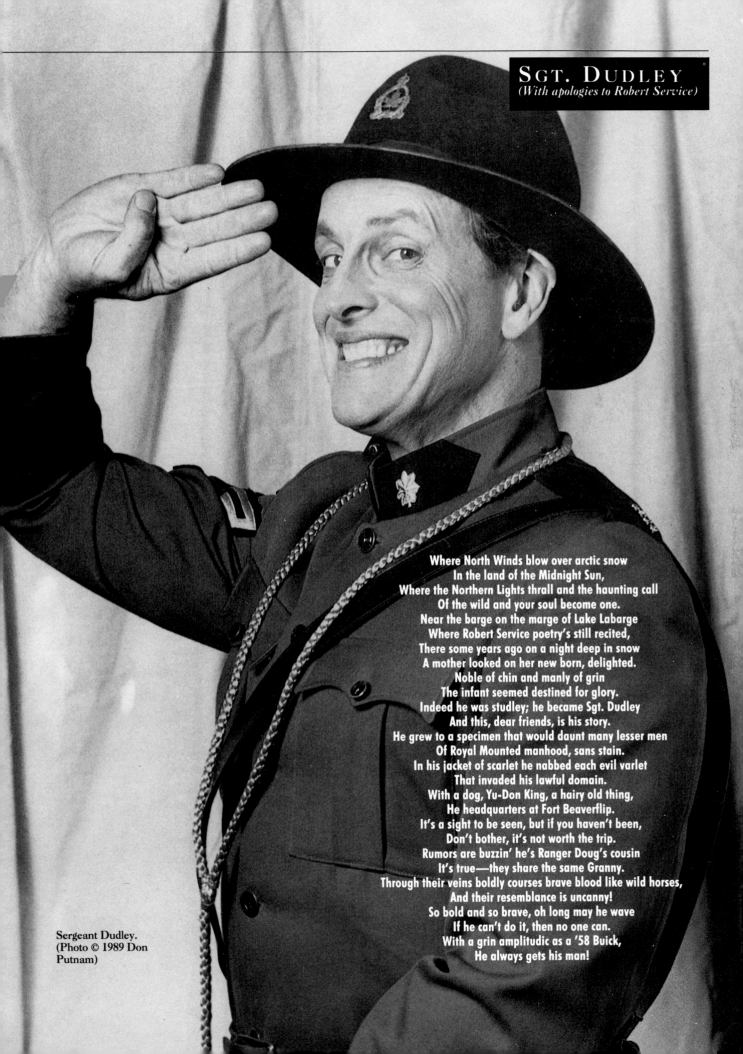

Where North Winds blow over arctic snow
In the land of the Midnight Sun,
Where the Northern Lights thrall and the haunting call
Of the wild and your soul become one.
Near the barge on the marge of Lake Labarge
Where Robert Service poetry's still recited,
There some years ago on a night deep in snow
A mother looked on her new born, delighted.
Noble of chin and manly of grin
The infant seemed destined for glory.
Indeed he was studley; he became Sgt. Dudley
And this, dear friends, is his story.
He grew to a specimen that would daunt many lesser men
Of Royal Mounted manhood, sans stain.
In his jacket of scarlet he nabbed each evil varlet
That invaded his lawful domain.
With a dog, Yu-Don King, a hairy old thing,
He headquarters at Fort Beaverflip.
It's a sight to be seen, but if you haven't been,
Don't bother, it's not worth the trip.
Rumors are buzzin' he's Ranger Doug's cousin
It's true—they share the same Granny.
Through their veins boldly courses brave blood like wild horses,
And their resemblance is uncanny!
So bold and so brave, oh long may he wave
If he can't do it, then no one can.
With a grin amplitudic as a '58 Buick,
He always gets his man!

Sergeant Dudley.
(Photo © 1989 Don
Putnam)

Photo © 1991 Peter Nash

Photo © 1990 Jim Hagans, TNN

21

FREDDIE LA
(IN HIS OWN WORDS)

Cowboys whoa! Like, today I saw some.

Their hats were outrageous, like totally awesome.

I'd been surfin' forever, but I thought about switchin',

Cause there goes these dudes lookin' totally bitchin'.

So I says to my chick, "Like I'm gonna go for it!"

And I scored this big hat, and like then I wore it!

I said, "Yo! check it out! It's like totally heavy!"

She goes, "Like, no way! You're like, from planet Debbie!"

But the cowboy kahuna goes like, "Ride along."

And like do cowboy stuff and like sing cowboy songs.

And he says it's way cool, I can still bring my board,

And my wax and my woodie and my little foot cord.

So, don't fence me in while I surf with the dogies,

And camp on the beach with my horse and my hobie.

Yo! I go with the flow and I dig Gene and Roy.

Cowabunga! Surf's up! I'm the surfin' cowboy!"

Freddie LA, the surfin' cowboy. (Photo © 1989 Don Putnam)

DOCTOR B. BAXTER BAZZLE AND MAMA

Dr. Bazzle, P.D., P.D.Q., R.F.D., Member National Geographic Society, and Mama are self-acknowledged universal experts on everything. They have had an extreme career on AM radio dispensing ludicrous advice to the lunatic fringe. A charming combination if there ever was one. Currently they are the exclusive pitch persons for Campfirelight Records (see p. 84)

FAMOUS BAZZLE(S) QUOTES:

"Ain't that right, mama?"
"That's right, Doctor Bazzle!"
"Sit down, Mama!"

H.H. "HAMMERHEAD" STILLSON

Hammerhead Stillson (the H.H. stands for H H) has the hardest cranium in the world. He earned his nickname in WW II while serving in the Army Corps of Engineers. When his unit found themselves supplied with everything but hammers and ordered to build a bridge across the Roan (not a misspelling) River in France, Hammerhead used his head and drove over ten thousand nails that day, completing the bridge just before errant friendly fire blew it up. These days he tours county fairs playing "Lady of Spain" on finely tuned railroad spikes while driving them into a slab of concrete. And with a head like that, he's a natural spokesperson for a variety of commercial products.

FAMOUS HAMMERHEAD QUOTES:

"Listen, Hoss, I didn't just fall off a turnip truck in the middle of New York City and land on my head . . . And even if I did it wouldn't hurt! Haw Haw Haw."

"With a head as hard as mine, if I ever went out of it I could never get back in."

SLOCUM & CHARLIE
(IN THEIR OWN WORDS)

(Slocum)
I've got a pencil thin mustache
And a reptilian demeanor
If I could squeeze a nickel from it
I'd take grandma to the cleaners.
I love forgery, extortion,
And changing cattle brands.
But, mostly I'm in love with very
Big and evil plans.
I want your coal and cattle, gold and timber,
And railroad right of way
I want your mineral rights, your water rights,
And air rights, by the way.
I love confiscation and intimidation
And owning all the land.
But, lately I've been gettin' into
Big and evil plans.

(Slocum & Charlie)
Because the plot demands
An evil man.
To prove the good are good
Someone's got to put them through it.
Even Shakespeare in his glory
Put good villains in his story.
It's a dirty job,
But someone's got to do it.

(Charlie)
Slocum, a brain like yours needs muscle
To make the action richer.
A brawny goon, a dark saloon,
Is why I'm in the picture.
Breaking arms and burning barns,
And springing you from the can,
Is why you need a guy like me
For big and evil plans.

(Slocum & Charlie)
Because the plot demands
An evil man.
To prove the good are good
Someone's got to put them through it.
Even Shakespeare in his glory
Put good villains in his story,
It's a dirty job,
But someone's got to do it.

Slocum and Charlie.
(Photo © 1991 Don Putnam)

Photo © 1992 Don Putnam

Photo © 1991 Peter Nash

SIDEMEAT

Creator of the hardest
substance known to man.
(Photo © 1989 Don
Putnam)

The Riders' faithful sidekick and
cook is the creator of the "Hardest
Substance Known To Man!" (See p.
38)

In addition to being a world-
reviled cook, Sidemeat is equally
reproachable for his social graces, and
is the current president of the "Gabby
Hayes Misogynist Society." But
despite all this, he has a heart of . . .
well, he has a heart. His mule is
named Senator, and why not?

FAMOUS SIDEMEAT QUOTES:

"Of course it's coffee!"
"Women."
"Mayhh, whew!"

MISTER LITERAL

A frequent guest on "Riders Radio Theater," Mister Literal is fighting a long, lonely battle against the insidious evils of careless conversation. He chairs the Department of Needless Nitpicking at the University of Wally Cox, and has published several almost-famous books.

ALMOST-FAMOUS BOOKS BY MISTER LITERAL:

"Everything I Need to Know I Learned in Kindergarten is Ridiculous!"

"English: Love It Or Shut Up!"

"Likes Music, Loves To Correct You."

"The Oxford Dictionary Of The English Language—Where Did It Go Wrong?"

TRADER DOUG AND THE FABULOUS BIRDS OF PARADISE

Trader Doug

Fred Ho

Woo Woo Wahine

Undoubtedly the most far-western band in existence, they are the mainstays of the Hoi Poi Loy Lounge in the Royal Jones Tourist Court in Honolulu, Hawaii. Their vibrant island music and the torrid hula hooping of the Woo Woo Wahine have—and it's no exaggeration to say this—stunned audiences for years. This is the sort of act that never fails to go unnoticed when it tours the mainland.

FAMOUS QUOTES:

"Hoopi hoopi hoopi!" Fred Ho, your Master of Ceremonies.

"Hi sailor." Woo Woo Wahine.

"No comment." Trader Doug.

L. Philo "Larry" Mammoth

Courtesy Texas Bix Bender

L. PHILO "LARRY" MAMMOTH

The last and worst of the B-Western movie producers. Long after anybody cared, he made a series of awful movies starring the astonishingly inept Art Smarm. After this failure he moved into late-night television huckstering and eventually wound up on an obscure public radio show selling everything from Prairie-Aire bottled water to correspondence courses in Self-Actualization Through Accordion Repair.

FAMOUS MAMMOTH QUOTES:

"Absolutely, incredibly, preposterously, unbelievably amazing!"

"If you're not completely, 100% satisfied with this product you're crazy!"

"Only $9.99!"

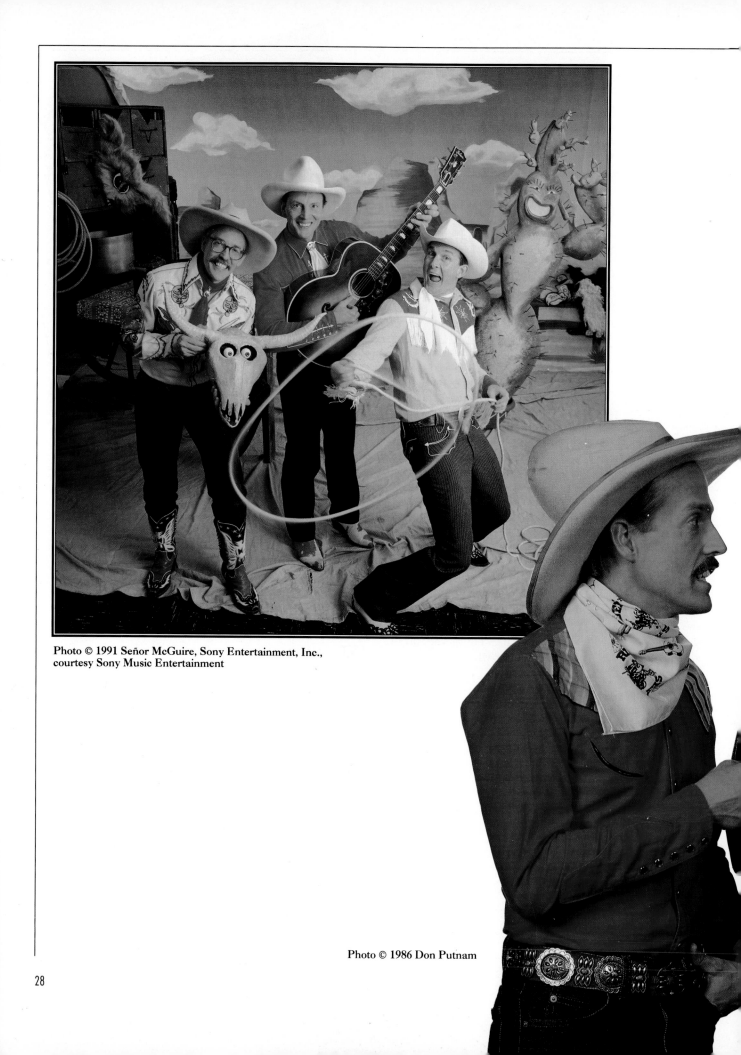

Photo © 1991 Señor McGuire, Sony Entertainment, Inc.,
courtesy Sony Music Entertainment

Photo © 1986 Don Putnam

28

Photo © 1989 Don Putnam

29

JOEY THE COWPOLKA KING

The Cowpolka King has in the past and to this day continues to perform with everyone from U-2 to Johnny Cash. However, in the opinion of every major music critic (of Slovenian descent) he reached the pinnacle of his career with the release of his steamy, torrid, lighthearted album "Perfume, Passion, and Polka!" The album is the culmination of his lifelong mania to turn every song into a polka. He began his career with a spectacular performance for the 1964 Presidential Inauguration. Unfortunately it went largely unnoticed as he was in Cleveland at the time. A subsequent thirty-year association with the legendary Frankie Yankovic led to the

Joey the Cowpolka King and Texas Bix Bender, in the alley behind the Emery Theater. (Photo by John Hughes)

The future Idol of American Youth, with a steely Rangerly gleam in his eye, age 5.

Ranger Doug.

30

development of his astonishing command of the descending diminished chords. This he now uses to beautifully stitch together the raveled seams of "Riders Radio Theater." Joey also makes frequent appearances with Riders In The Sky on the road and in his spare time enjoys manipulating the stock market just to hear it squeal.

BIG ZENO CLINKER

"The Big Banger" is a sound-effects wizard par excellence. He is also a former U. S. Commissioner of Civil Oaths. He began his career on "Riders Radio Theater" as a snaffle mender and quickly advanced to the coveted job of SFX (radio gibberish for "sound effects") wrangler. In his spare time he is a junior partner in the firm of Zeno Clinker & Associate (deceased).

RANGER DOUG

"The Idol Of American Youth" wears a big hat and has a big smile, reminiscent of the grill of a '58 Buick. His voice and big guitar have set many a feminine heart aflutter. His extraordinary yodel is as smooth as a well-worn saddle, faster than a speeding bullet, and more powerful than a locomotive. His horse is named Turbo, "The Wonder Horse of the West."

THE FAIR ROBERTA

The fair Roberta is the Art Director and Production Foreman on "Riders Radio Theater." (Under the pseudonym "Campfire Bert" she also manages Too Slim's Mercantile. She helps keep us on time, on the trail, and can even find Woody Paul when no one else can. Her fan club's motto is "She's more than fair," and they're more than right.

TOO SLIM

"The Man Of Many Hats" is a licensed driver and virtuoso on the bunkhouse face. He plays the upright bass and sings pretty darn well, too. He knows the Boy Scout oath frontwards and backwards, he's the fastest quip in the West, and is a proud supporter and continuing sponsor of "The Greater Cincinnati Comedians For Quayle Committee." His horse is named Argyle.

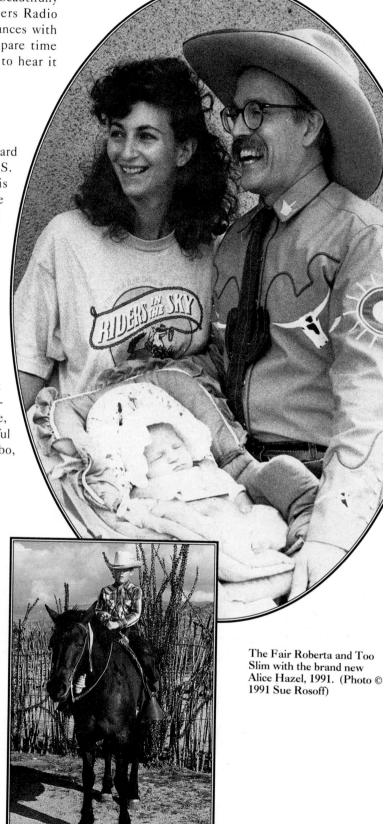

The Fair Roberta and Too Slim with the brand new Alice Hazel, 1991. (Photo © 1991 Sue Rosoff)

Too Slim, 1956. Born to the saddle.

31

Photo © 1991 David Skepner

When Joey was with the trail drive.
(Photo © 1991 Peter Nash)

WOODY PAUL

"The King Of The Cowboy Fiddlers" is a true Renaissance man. He is a serious singer/songwriter, part-time brain surgeon (unlicensed), and occasional unemployable rocket scientist. He also holds advanced rope-waxing degrees from Polymorphic U. and M.I.T. (Montana Institute of Technology.) His keen scientific mind is also neat and peachy. He hates horses and drives a Yugo on trail drives and roundups.

TEXAS BIX BENDER

The legendary border radio announcer is known as "The Voice That Sold A Million Baby Chicks." He won his fame as an ace pilot of the airwaves broadcasting from radio station XEGG, which was located in romantic Old Mexico just across the silvery Rio Grande from Del Rio, Texas. XEGG scoured the ether with an unsurpassed effective transmitting power of one-and-a-half million watts! It could be heard from Texas to Tokyo. And, thanks to occasional atmospheric conditions and the ozone skip effect, live baby chicks have been ordered from as far away as Katmandu and Samarkand. Cowboys riding the range in West Texas have even reported that the signal was so strong they didn't even need a radio to pick it up. At night, when they bedded down they would fall asleep to the voice of Texas Bix Bender humming through the barbed wire! (This invariably led to an undeniable urge on their part to give up cowboying and go into the chicken business, which many of them did. This explains the large number of chicken ranches in West Texas to this day.)

Woody Paul. (Photo © 1991 Sue Rosoff)

The young Woody Paul. You can see that cowboyin' is nothing new to him.

"Get Ready" for a spectacular rope trick.

The Python. Notice how the rope coils up the arm
—a favorite in Brazil.

The Helicopter. You can almost hear the traffic report.

Spinning the shape of Texas . . .

. . . and jumping through!

Oh, no—a panther! No problem!

What a fighter!

Nice work, Pop! (Photo series courtesy Woody Paul)

DON'T MISS THIS *ONCE-IN-A-LIFETIME* CHANCE TO LIVE YOUR DREAMS!
The tuition is only $9.99 down and $9.99 a month until you graduate.*

Act now and we'll include, absolutely free, a graduate course in words to mumble as you mill around in a crowd scene. (As a classically trained geezer there's a lot more you can say than just "Rhubarb rhubarb rhubarb" or "Peas and carrots, peas and carrots, peas and carrots.")

ENROLLMENT IS UNLIMITED, SO DON'T WAIT! HAVE YOUR VISA, ALBANIAN EXPRESS, OR MASTERCARD READY AND CALL 1-900-GEEZERS! DO IT NOW AND SOON HOLLYWOOD WILL BE CALLING YOU!!!

(GEEZERETTE COURSES ALSO AVAILABLE FOR ADVENTUROUS *BUCKARETTES!*)

*M.V.G.C.C. will graduate no Geezer before he's properly aged. Therefore, the curriculum runs from four to forty years.

A Side of Cooking
by Sidemeat

Folks are always asking me what on earth I do to food when I cook it. How do I get those unusual colors, those woolly textures, and those fulsome flavors? Well, it ain't easy, but if you follow the recipes I'm about to give you and use my secret ingredients, you can do it, too.

Now, all a good cook needs to know about are the three basic food groups, biscuits, beans, and coffee. And here's how to fix 'em!

ROCK BISCUITS
(The Hardest Substance Known To Man)

The great thing about these biscuits is that they're so hard to eat that nobody wants more than one and so each batch you cook up lasts a long, long time. And what's more, any uneaten ones can be used as doorstops, building blocks, gravel crushers, diamond cutters, nutcrackers, and the like.

10 Pounds flour

1 Pound baking soda

1/2 Pound salt

5 Pounds grease (#80 weight axle grease is best)

1 Pound Portland #9 cement

1 Pound my secret ingredient (Sand—it puts a little grit in your craw)

4 4x4s

Mix all the ingredients except the 4x4s in a big bowl, then add a fair amount of liquid (water, milk, coffee, whatever you've got handy) and stir it up for 15 or 20 seconds—that's all it takes—you want it good and lumpy. Next, scoop it up by the handful and plop it down onto a piece of sheet iron. Bake it on as high a heat as you've got for five or six hours. Now, THIS IS VERY IMPORTANT! I don't care how sturdy a table you've got in your kitchen, take those 4x4s the recipe calls for and shore up that table, because, believe me—when you take that piece of sheet iron with those biscuits on it out of the oven and drop it on that table you'll thank your lucky stars for those 4x4s.

Serves more than anybody can, or ever will, eat.

JAVA JOE

A cowboy will ride a long way for a good cup of coffee, but what do they know? Gourmets like you and me cannot be bothered by the likes and dislikes of the dull palates of the average cowboy. We need a strong, robust, rich cup of coffee that can stand on its own. And here's the recipe for it.

2 Pounds of coffee beans

1 Gallon of water

1 #10 can of axle grease (80 weight is best here as well)

1 Horseshoe

Put the coffee beans in a gunny sack and beat them mercilessly with a ball-peen hammer for 5 full minutes. Next, put the battered beans in a big coffee pot, add the water, dump in the axle grease, and toss in the horseshoe. Put the pot on the fire and forget about it for the next 4 or 5 days. Then check on it and if the horseshoe is floating it's done. Otherwise, continue to cook it until the horseshoe floats. Then, call in the hands and start twisting off cups of the stoutest joe on this planet.

Serves more than anybody will want.

MARIAH BEANS

My beans are justly famous all over the West. Why the cowboys have even written a song about them. It goes like this:

"Away out here they named my grub
While sitting 'round the fire.
The coffee's Joe, the biscuit's Rock,
And they call my beans Mariah.
Mariah, Mariah,
They call my beans Mariah.
Mariah is the wind that blows
Around the campfire nightly."

Well, that's enough of that. I'm sure you get the picture. No need to get to the part where "the men are out there dying." Here's the recipe, and like all true culinary masterpieces it's simple and easy to fix.

10 Pounds of dried pinto beans

1 Quart of grease (Need I even have to say that 80 weight axle grease is best?)

5 Pounds of fatback

Put the beans in a big pot. (No need to rinse and sort as the axle grease and cooking time will soften and disintegrate anything on what's left of God's green planet.) Add the water, axle grease, and fatback. Put the pot on the fire and let it boil heartily for two full weeks—add water as needed.

Serve with biscuits, coffee, and heaping portions of Di-gel.

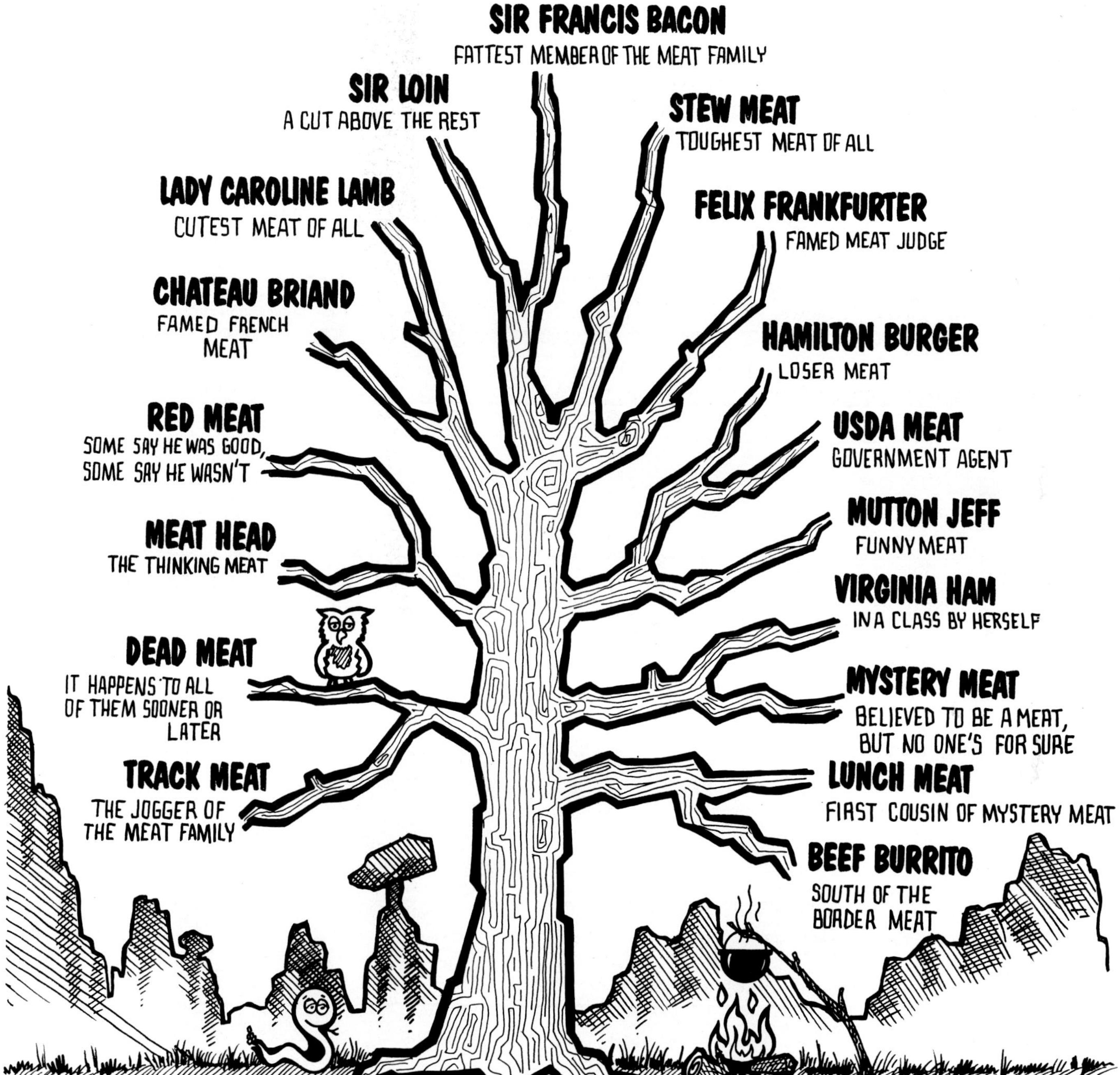

SIR FRANCIS BACON
FATTEST MEMBER OF THE MEAT FAMILY

SIR LOIN
A CUT ABOVE THE REST

STEW MEAT
TOUGHEST MEAT OF ALL

LADY CAROLINE LAMB
CUTEST MEAT OF ALL

FELIX FRANKFURTER
FAMED MEAT JUDGE

CHATEAU BRIAND
FAMED FRENCH MEAT

HAMILTON BURGER
LOSER MEAT

RED MEAT
SOME SAY HE WAS GOOD, SOME SAY HE WASN'T

USDA MEAT
GOVERNMENT AGENT

MEAT HEAD
THE THINKING MEAT

MUTTON JEFF
FUNNY MEAT

VIRGINIA HAM
IN A CLASS BY HERSELF

DEAD MEAT
IT HAPPENS TO ALL OF THEM SOONER OR LATER

MYSTERY MEAT
BELIEVED TO BE A MEAT, BUT NO ONE'S FOR SURE

TRACK MEAT
THE JOGGER OF THE MEAT FAMILY

LUNCH MEAT
FIRST COUSIN OF MYSTERY MEAT

BEEF BURRITO
SOUTH OF THE BORDER MEAT

THE MEAT FAMILY TREE

With Roy Rogers on "Hee Haw." (Photo © 1988 Don Putnam)

With Pam Tillis on "Riders Radio Theater." (Photo © David Skepner)

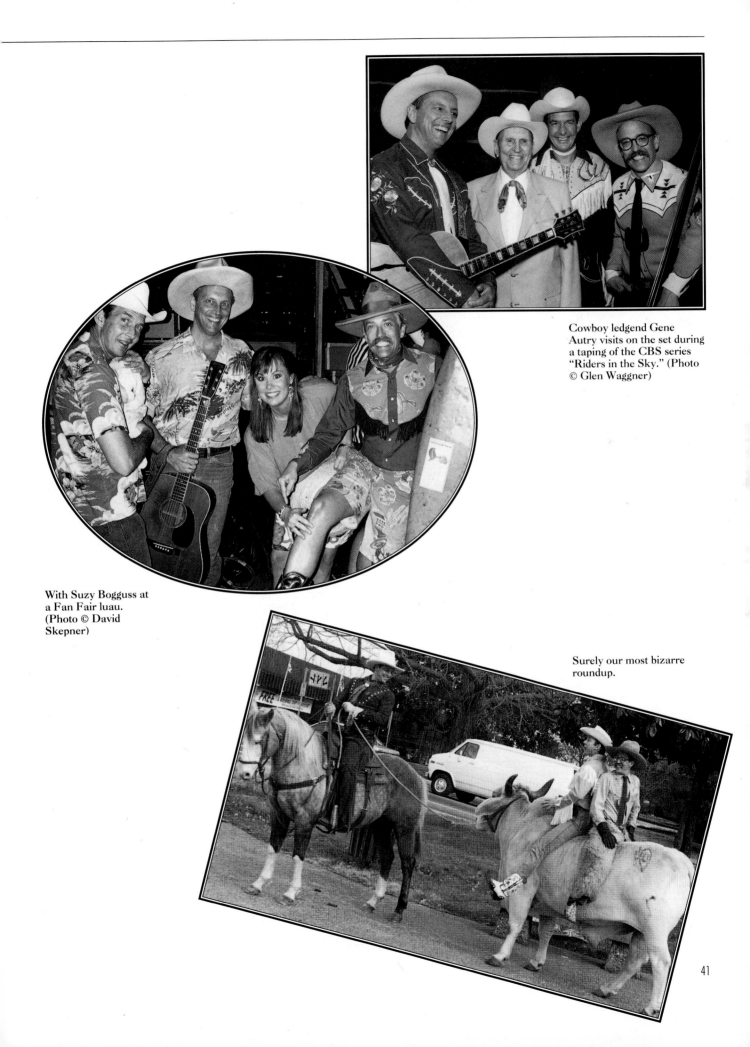

Cowboy ledgend Gene
Autry visits on the set during
a taping of the CBS series
"Riders in the Sky." (Photo
© Glen Waggner)

With Suzy Bogguss at
a Fan Fair luau.
(Photo © David
Skepner)

Surely our most bizarre
roundup.

41

Ranger Doug and son,
Jamie, CBS lot, 1991.
(Photo © 1991 Sue Rosoff)

Great boots! Thanks to the
critters who gave their lives
for these. Woody Paul (left)
and Jerry Jeff Walker.
(Photo © 1991 Sue Rosoff)

Woody Paul with his kids,
Jacob and Rebecca, CBS
lot, 1991. (Photo © 1991
Sue Rosoff)

Riders host "Nashville Now." Ranger Doug attempts to restore order as the evil twins of Minnie Pearl and Ralph Emery try to wrest the show from his control. (Photo © David Skepner)

Woody Paul, Don Edwards, Ranger Doug, Too Slim, and Jerry Jeff Walker jam at the Cowboy Poetry Gathering in Elko, 1987. (Photo © 1991 Sue Rosoff)

Ranger Doug and Too Slim
with Sony Music / Nashville
president Roy Wunsch, his
wife, Mary Ann, and
manager David Skepner.

With Waylen Jennings and
Jessi Colter at a hospital
Hospitality House benefit
show, 1989. (Photo © 1992
David Skepner)

With Michael Martin
Murphey (center) during a
taping of "Riders Radio
Theater." At far left is "Iron
Man" Kevin Kenworthy
(The Nashville Network).
(Photo © 1991 David
Skepner)

Riders' style appeals to all ages. (Photo © 1991 Sue Rosoff)

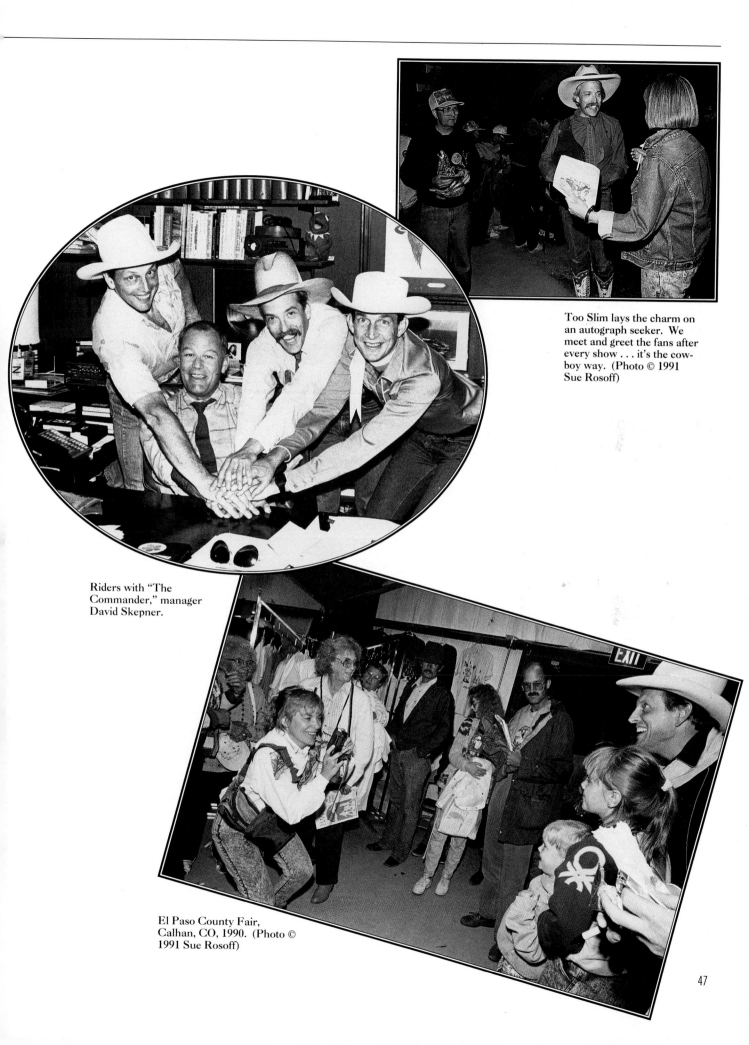

Too Slim lays the charm on an autograph seeker. We meet and greet the fans after every show . . . it's the cowboy way. (Photo © 1991 Sue Rosoff)

Riders with "The Commander," manager David Skepner.

El Paso County Fair, Calhan, CO, 1990. (Photo © 1991 Sue Rosoff)

Too Slim with kids, Calhan,
CO, 1990. (Photo © 1991
Sue Rosoff)

Impromptu session in the
mezzanine at Stockman's in
Elko. (Photo © 1991 Sue
Rosoff)

Riders in the Sky perform the national anthem at Riverfront Stadium prior to a 1991 Cincinnati Reds baseball game. (Photo © 1991 David Skepner)

RIDERS RADIO THEATER

"Riders Radio Theater" in progress, with Big Zeno Clinker SFXing in the background and Texas Bix announcing on the right. Can you tell Too Jaws from Too Slim? (Courtesy Texas Bix Bender)

RIDERS RADIO THEATER WAS A PHRASE COINED by Tumbleweed Tommy Goldsmith during his brief tenure as a Rider In The Sky. It described a series of skits written by Too Slim and performed by the Riders as part of their stage act in the early days of their career. As the Riders' act matured, they dropped the skits and concentrated on refining their various characters and developing a less structured, freer-flowing comedic style. But the concept was not forgotten, and several years later, in 1984, at the instigation of Bruce Nemerov, the idea was revived during an extended lunch at a now-defunct Nashville restaurant. Present that fateful day were Woody Paul, Too Slim, Ranger Doug, Bruce, Ned Ramage, and Texas Bix Bender. Bruce had contacted American Public Radio and they had shown a strong interest in a Riders In The Sky program. Everyone at the table that day thought it was a pretty good idea, too, and Too Slim knew exactly where to begin. Reaching into an inner pocket of his jacket, he produced a couple of yellowed, dog-eared pages of an early Riders Radio Theater skit called "Dialing For Dogies!"

Rehearsing for "Riders Radio Theater" with Martin Del Ray. (Photo by Jim Springfield)

The stage is set for "Riders Radio Theater." (Photo by Jim Springfield)

and Texas Bix at the microphones, radio history was made . . . and almost instantly forgotten.

American Public Radio heard the pilot, liked it, was even enthusiastic about it; but when they took it to their board for financing, it was rejected on the grounds it lacked any classical music content. Well, they had us there. (Though many who love the poetry, romance, and beauty in the music and lyrics of Bob Nolan, Tim Spencer, Stan Jones, Billy Hill, and Riders In The Sky would righteously argue the point.)

Then, in January 1988, The Riders were preparing to do their second MCA album. (Riders In The Sky were the first western music group to be on a major record label in over twenty years.) Since their first MCA album had primarily been music, it was decided that this one would be mostly comedy. Thus, Riders Radio Theater was reborn on vinyl. Texas Bix Bender was contacted and agreed to participate in the writing and serve as announcer on the record. Most of the material had its genesis with Too Slim driving and

Well, who could argue with a title like that? A story conference followed, at which a format, enlarged plotline, and other particulars were worked out. Then Texas Bix took all these elements and hammered them into a thirty-minute script for a pilot show. Shortly after that a small band of extremely faithful fans were lured with the promise of free food and drink to Tom T. Hall's Toybox Recording Studio in Brentwood, Tennessee. There, with Bruce Nemerov at the controls and Riders In The Sky

Carin Joy sells Too Slim's
Mercantile in the lobby.
(Photo by John Hughes)

diately Doctor J. C. King and Larry Ashcraft at Public Radio station WVXU in Cincinnati stepped in, and the Queen City of the West (as it was so designated by no less a light than Henry Wadsworth Longfellow, 1807–1882, in his ode to "Catawba Wine") became the new home for Riders Radio Theater.

Now, every month or so, The Riders, Joey, Big Zeno, and Texas Bix mount up and launch a trail drive north to the historic Emory Theater in downtown Cincinnati, where they play to wonderful, enthusiastic, capacity crowds who saddle up again and again and ride the airwaves with Riders In The Sky!

At the time of this writing the future of "Riders Radio Theater" is up in the air. (Pun intended. Sorry, Ranger Doug.) To do a show of this nature is a big drain on any public radio station's resources and also requires a terrific amount of time and work for little financial return on the part of the writers and performers. But several avenues are being explored and it is everybody's desire—including The Riders', Texas Bix, Joey, Big Zeno, WVXU, and WPLN, along with a lot of incredibly loyal and dedicated fans all across America and Australia—to keep "Riders Radio Theater" on the air!

One of the most popular features on "Riders Radio Theater" is the ongoing saga of "The Cowboy Way," a serial melodrama that features heroic derring-do of mythic proportions, unredeemable villainy such as hasn't been since the days of Simon LeGree, astounding plots to rival those of the most outrageous pulps, and a degree of silliness and outrageous fun not heard of since the BBC's great "Goon Shows" of the 1950s. In these fantastic and funny stories, Riders In The Sky and the good but goofy citizens of Tumbleweed Valley do battle with the "prince of villains," A. Swinburne Slocum, and his henchman, Charlie. This pair of moral morons are continually up to their dirty necks in big and evil plans that involve everything from using toxic wastes to poison the Los Angeles water supply (so they can make a fortune selling "Prairie Aire" bottled water to thirsty Angelenos), to sabotaging the Alaskan Pipeline with a death ray so they can make a fortune in oil futures. (These polecats, like most other varmints in the '90s, are only in it for the money.)

Powered by timely, witty, well-written scripts that positively refuse to take themselves seriously, these fast-paced cliffhangers zip blithely along at a real laugh-a-minute pace. Each episode features the dramatic, vivid, tongue-firmly-in-cheek narration of Texas Bix Bender, the sound effects wizardry of the inimitable Big Zeno Clinker, the always on-the-mark accordion artistry of Joey the Cowpolka King, and of course, the marvelous characterizations and quick wit of Riders In The Sky.

Texas Bix riding shotgun as the Riders bus rolled along the back roads of Texas in between show dates.

The album was recorded in Nashville on March 6, 7, and 8 and released to rave notices, including one in *People* magazine. Shortly after that WPLN, Public Radio in Nashville, got involved, and in no time the words of Texas Bix Bender were heard from coast to coast proclaiming that "Riders Radio Theater is on the air!"

The first few shows were a little rocky. But with the addition of sound-effects wizard Big Zeno Clinker and the show's secret weapon, Joey the Cowpolka King, the show hit its stride.

But after the first year, despite having created a nationwide network of over a hundred public radio stations in America and Australia, WPLN elected not to continue their relationship with the show. Almost imme-

—ANNOUNCING—

THE HOME VERSION OF

"RIDERS RADIO THEATER!"

Yes! Now, in the privacy of your own home, you, your family and friends can produce, direct, and star in your very own production of the exciting western melodrama "Mystery of the Lost Ozone"! What's that, you say? There're only two or three or four persons residing in your home (that you know about) and one of them is a Scientologist? No problem! There are only three Riders In The Sky (and one of them is a nuclear physicist) and only one Texas Bix Bender (that we know about). So how do we do it? Simple! With reckless abandon each player takes on more than one role (except for Texas Bix Bender), and you can, too! For example, when this melodrama was originally performed on Riders Radio Theater:

RANGER DOUG played himself and Charlie.

TOO SLIM played himself, the record-store clerk, and Marilyn Quayle.

WOODY PAUL played himself and Dan Quayle.

TEXAS BIX BENDER, as far as we know, played himself.

If you divide the roles in a similar manner for your production (i.e., whoever plays Ranger Doug plays Charlie, whoever plays Too Slim plays Slocum and Marilyn Quayle, etc.), you will find that the script, for the most part, is structured so that you won't have the same actor having to carry on a conversation between two different characters both of whom are himself. (Get the Scientologist to explain this to you, but tell him not to jump to any forgone conclusions.)

Special Note: Two very important spokes in the "Riders Radio Theater" wheel are Joey the Cowpolka King, accordion artiste extraordinaire, and Big Zeno Clinker, sound-effects master of the air. So, in addition to the various characters in the script, someone will also have to handle their chores, as well. Wherever there is an "Sfx" (radio gibberish for sound effect), following it will be a Big Zeno Secret, giving you the inside poop on how Big Z himself would do it. Similarly, wherever there is a "Joey" cue, unless it is immediately obvious what to do, right beneath it will be a "Joey Note" with a suggestion as to what to do.

(First Joey Note: If there's not an accordion in the house, shame! But until you can remedy the situation, the designated accordion player can get by with some clever humming.)

"MYSTERY OF THE LOST OZONE"

Cast of Characters

RANGER DOUG—The Idol of American Youth, strong and stalwart, with a voice like Clayton Moore as The Lone Ranger.

TOO SLIM—Virtuous, loyal, and highly impressionable, with a voice like a middle-aged Boy Scout.

WOODY PAUL—A cross between Albert Einstein and Jethro Clampett, with a voice somewhere in between.

TEXAS BIX BENDER—A deep, dramatic voice that always knows what's going on and doesn't mind telling you . . . and telling you . . . and . . .

SIDEMEAT—The Riders' cranky ol' sidekick who has a voice reminiscent of Gabby Hayes.

A. SWINBURNE SLOCUM—A totally unprincipled scoundrel, with a voice like a late-night-TV Ginzu knife pitchman.

CHARLIE—A solid three-hundred-pound doofus, with a menacing voice and a brutal demeanor.

CLERK IN RECORD STORE—Typical arrogant record-store clerk, with a voice like Pee Wee Herman.

DAN QUAYLE—A voice like a teen-age Alfalfa.

MARILYN QUAYLE—A voice like a young Julia Child.

BIG ZENO'S SOUND EFFECTS LIST
(You might want to gather these items and have them handy before show time.)

A plastic cup or a hammer.

A calculator or hand-held video game that beeps when you press a button.

A telephone extension—disconnected.

The Script

(Joey: Hums "Riders Radio Theater Theme.")

Texas Bix (over humming)

And now, "Riders Radio Theater" presents the ongoing saga of "The Cowboy Way." Tonight, the exciting western melodrama, "Mystery of the Lost Ozone!" As faithful listeners will no doubt recall, Riders In The Sky have been in Hollywood for the past three months working on their big television show. As we join them now, they are just coming through Grapevine Pass and entering Tumbleweed Valley.

(Joey stops humming.)

(Sfx: horses' hooves walking.)

(Big Zeno Secret: pat hands rhythmically on chest or, if you have them, beat coconut shells against your head or a tabletop.)

Texas Bix

Suddenly a prairie dog spooks their horses!

(Joey: Sting.)

(Joey Note: "Sting" is musician gibberish for a dramatic "Da dah!")

(Sfx: Horse neighs wildly.)

(Big Zeno Secret: Laugh like Walter Brennan.)

Ranger Doug

Whoa Turbo!

Too Slim

Easy Argyle!

Woody Paul

Whoa, Yugo!

Too Slim

Wait a minute, Texas Bix, horses aren't afraid of prairie dogs.

Texas Bix

They are when they're ten feet tall.

Too Slim

Ten feet tall! Wow!

Woody Paul

This is weird.

Texas Bix

Yes, and almost immediately an even weirder event occurs—forty ducks come crashing down on them from out of the sky!

(Sfx: Waaaaak! Crash! Waaaaak! Crash! Waaaaak! Crash!)

(Big Zeno Secret: Just say it like it's written and the three times indicated should do it, but if you're a purist or having fun with it, go ahead and repeat "waaaaak! crash!" 37 more times.)

Too Slim

Good grief! Where did these ducks come from?

Ranger Doug

And why did they come crashing down on us out of nowhere?

Too Slim

At least they're not hurt too bad.

Woody Paul

Yeah, they'll be all right, they're just stunned. But this is really getting weird.

Texas Bix

And it gets weirder. As the Riders approach a small highway shopping center, they notice something very, very wrong.

Too Slim

Look! The tanning salon has gone out of business! I had ten visits left on my card, too!

Woody Paul

What in the world is going on around here?

Ranger Doug

Let's head for home. Maybe Sidemeat can give us some answers.

Ranger Doug, Too Slim, Woody Paul

Hyanh! Get up there!

(Sfx: Horses gallop off.)

(Joey: Hum fast galloping music.)

Texas Bix

Urgently, Riders In The Sky spur their trusty mounts on, and in no time they arrive at their home on the range, the famed ol' Harmony Ranch. There, over a cup of coffee at the kitchen table, Sidemeat fills them in on what's been going on . . .

Sidemeat

Nyah, whew! It's been really weird around here for the last two or three months. Ten-feet-tall prairie dogs roaming the range scaring livestock and digging the biggest holes you ever seen . . . nobody knows where they come from. Ducks have pretty much quit flying over the valley, and when they do they always crash and have to walk out . . . Who needs more coffee?

Ranger Doug

I'll risk another cup.

Sidemeat

Okay, I'll pour and you twist 'er off when your cup's full.

(Sfx: Glug, glug, glug—sound of very thick coffee twisted off.)

(Big Zeno Secret: To get the coffee-twisting sound, squeeze your hands slowly around a smooth, dry plastic cup or the handle on a hammer.)

Ranger Doug

Thanks, Side.

Too Slim

Side, what happened to the tanning salons?

Sidemeat

Nobody needs 'em anymore. Sun's so strong it tans you right through your clothes! Everybody has to use this industrial-strength sunblock called "Coppertone to the Bone."

Woody Paul

Hmm, mutant prairie dogs, disoriented ducks, sunburns through your clothes . . . it almost sounds like there's a hole in the ozone right over Tumbleweed Valley.

Too Slim

Gosh, what could be causing it?

Woody Paul

I don't know.

Ranger Doug

I don't either, Woody, but I don't have to. What I do know is that when something weird is stirring in Tumbleweed Valley you can usually find the tainted hand of a certain rat with a pencil mustache stirring it up.

All

(Gasp) Slocum!!!

Ranger Doug

Boys, I think we'd better ride into town and have a look around.

Sidemeat

I'll go with you. It'll give me a chance to pick up a book I ordered a while back.

Woody Paul

What book?

Sidemeat

It's called *Eat What You Cook And Like It Through Hypnotism.* Nyah, whew!

Woody Paul

It'll take more than hypnotism to pull that off.

Sidemeat

Oh yeah, without a doubt, but . . . say! Why you . . . !

R. Doug

Easy, Side. C'mon, we'd better get going. When we get there, while you get your book we'll nose around and see if anybody's seen Slocum or Charlie lately.

Woody Paul & Too Slim

Great idea, Ranger Doug!

Ranger Doug

Thanks, boys. It's that kinda thinking that's made me the Idol of American Youth.

(Joey: Hum Slocum and Charlie's theme song, "Someone's Got To Do It," or some other properly sinister tune.)

Texas Bix (over humming)

While Riders In The Sky make plans to go to Tumbleweed City and seek clues as to the whereabouts of Slocum and Charlie, the subjects of their curiosity are making plans of their own, big and evil plans.

(Joey: Stop humming.)

Slocum

Okay, Charlie, give it three good blasts! (Laughs evilly.)

Charlie

Right.

(Sfx: Very loud psst! psst! psst!)

(Big Zeno Secret: You're imitating the sound of a fifty-foot-tall aerosol can being sprayed, so do it loud and through cupped hands.)

Slocum

Okay, that should do it. Now it's time for me to make "the" phone call. While I'm doing that, I want you to ride into town and pick me up a copy of *Slim Whitman's Greatest Hits, Volume 19* on CD.

Charlie

Huh? Why d'ya want me to do that, boss?

Slocum

Because that's the one he yodels on.

Charlie

Oh.

Slocum

Here's twenty bucks, now get going.

Charlie

Right.

(Sfx: Footsteps to door, door opens, door closes.)

(Big Zeno Secret: Walk over to a door, open and close it.)

Slocum

Okay, now, to make "the" call to the Chairman of the President's Commission on the Ozone. (Laughs evilly again.)

(Sfx: Five numbers on phone being punched.)

(Big Zeno Secret: Use a calculator, a hand-held video game, or a phone.)

(Big Zeno Secret: Be sure to disconnect an extension if you use one.)

Dan Quayle

(Talk through cupped hands to simulate answering machine.)

Hi! You've reached BR-549, that number again is BR-549. This is your vice-president . . . *your* vice-president. Neither Marilyn nor I can come to the phone right now, no. Because you know why? Because we're attending a very important month-long government conference in Palm Springs on the homeless. That's right, the homeless—why? Because we care, that's why. But because we care about our jobs, too, you know what we do? We check our answering machine very regularly. So if you'll leave a message we'll get right back to you. I mean it.

(Sfx: beep.)

(Big Zeno Secret: Use whatever you used for the phone, but only punch it once.)

Slocum

That's quite a heartfelt message, Danny boy. Now here's one for you! The world is gonna end tomorrow! (That evil laugh again.) I'm gonna destroy the ozone layer all over the world unless you meet my demands! And here they are: I want ten billion dollars in gold bullion. Uh, I want the heat off my buddy Noriega, and, uh, I want Jim and Tammy to get the PTL back, and, oh yeah! I want Pete Rose made the commissioner of baseball. On top of all that I want a Stealth Bomber . . . uh, naw, I want something that'll really fly, make it a 1972 Plymouth Roadrunner and I want a full tank of gas in it, too! Get all that together by tomorrow night or it's bye-bye planet earth! Well, its been good talking with you, Junior. I'll call you back tomorrow morning with delivery details. So long for now! (Evil laugh again.)

(Sfx: Phone hung up.)

(Joey: Big sting.)

(Joey Note: A big sting is a loud, fast "Duh duh duh dum!)

Texas Bix

A short time after Slocum's ominous phone call, Riders In The Sky arrive in Tumbleweed City and ride down Rex Allen Boulevard.

(Sfx: Horses' hooves.)

Sidemeat

Nyah, there's Sagebrush Sam's Book and Record Emporium. That's where my book is.

Ranger Doug

Okay, Side, we'll meet you over by the . . .

Woody Paul

Wait a minute, Ranger Doug! Isn't that Charlie just going into Sagebrush Sam's?

Ranger Doug

It sure is, Woody! C'mon boys, let's leave the horses at that hitching post and go have a little talk with Mister Charlie.

(Joey: Hum a little segue.)

(Joey Note: Try a soft, slow, "Duh duh duh dum!")

Texas Bix

Meanwhile, inside Sagebrush Sam's Book and Record Emporium . . .

Charlie

Uh, say bud . . .

Clerk

Say what?

Charlie

I'm looking for a Slim Whitman CD.

Clerk

Who isn't. You'll find all his albums, tapes, and CDs in our special Slim Whitman Annex. It's through that curtain back there to your left.

Charlie

Right.

Clerk

No, man, left.

Charlie

Left what?

Clerk

That way, man . . . go, go, I got work to do.

Charlie

Right.

Clerk

Yeah, right.

(Joey: Hum same little segue as above—"Da da da dum!")

Texas Bix

As Charlie makes his way back to the Slim Whitman Annex, Riders In The Sky enter Sagebrush Sam's.

Too Slim

Look! Isn't that Charlie going into the Slim Whitman Annex?

Woody Paul

It sure is!

Ranger Doug

Let's go have a little talk with that hombre.

Sidemeat

Nyah, you boys go ahead. I'm gonna go get my book and I'll meet you there.

Ranger Doug

Okay, Side. C'mon boys!

(Joey: hum a short segue.)

Texas Bix

Quickly, the Riders make their way through the store and through the curtains of the annex where they see one lone shopper.

Charlie (to himself)

Gee, there's so many . . . here it is! Hmm . . . the boss gave me a twenty, but he said to "pick it up" . . . I guess that means I keep the twenty and just pick up the CD and put it in my pocket. Heh, heh, heh.

Ranger Doug

That's shoplifting, Charlie.

Charlie

Huh? Naw it isn't. It's a Slim Whitman record. Say, what are you guys doing here?

Too Slim

Arresting you for shoplifting!

Charlie

You'll never make it stick, pinhead.

Ranger Doug

Acting bad won't help you, Charlie.

Charlie

Yeah, well don't you think you're overplaying it a bit yourself?

Ranger Doug

What's going on in this valley, Charlie? What's Slocum up to?

Charlie

How should I know.

Sidemeat (coming from off mic.)

Nyah, what the dingbustus is going on back here!

Woody Paul

Charlie won't talk.

Sidemeat

Is that right, Charlie?

Charlie

That's right, meathead.

Sidemeat

Nyah, beat it out of him, Ranger Doug!

Ranger Doug

That would be the easy way, Sidemeat, but . . .

Sidemeat

That again. Wait! I know! I'll hypnotize him! I've been glancing over this book I just got and I bet I can do it!

Charlie

You can't hypnotize me . . . I'm getting outta here!

Ranger Doug (grabs Charlie)

Hold it, Charlie!

Charlie

Ungh! Lemme go!

Ranger Doug

Okay, Side, give it a try.

Sidemeat

Look into my eyes, Charlie.

Charlie

No . . . I . . .

Sidemeat

You're getting very, very sleepy. Right?

Charlie

Right . . . zzzzzzzzzzzzzz.

Sidemeat

Whew! This guy's a tough subject.

Woody Paul

Yeah, but he's finally under. What are you gonna do now?

Sidemeat

Uh, okay, Charlie, act like a chicken.

Charlie

Buck, buc, buc, buc. Buck, buc, buc, buc.

Ranger Doug

Good job, Sidemeat, but that's not helping us much.

Sidemeat

Oh, all right. Charlie, we're gonna ask you some questions and you'll answer them truthfully, no lies, you got that?

Charlie

Right.

Ranger Doug

Charlie, what is Slocum up to?

Charlie

He's built a giant aerosol can up in Thieves Canyon and he's been testing it over Tumbleweed Valley.

Too Slim

That's what's happened! He's destroying the ozone over the valley!

Ranger Doug

Why Charlie?

Charlie

To prove he can do it. To prove he can do the "big blast."

Woody Paul

What's the "big blast?"

Charlie

If Dan Quayle doesn't meet his blackmail demands by tomorrow night, Slocum is gonna destroy the ozone layer all over the world.

Sidemeat

You mean it's up to Dan Quayle to deal with this?

Too Slim

That's good to know.

Woody Paul

Yeah, he'll know what to do.

Ranger Doug

Hold on there, boys. Sure it would be the easy way to just sit back and leave it to Dan to deal with the total destruction of the ozone and the world as we know it. Yes, that would be the easy way, but . . .

Riders

It wouldn't be the cowboy way!

Ranger Doug

Wake him up, Side, then let's all go pay a little call on Mister Slocum.

Sidemeat

All right, but we may need this jasper again, so before I do, I'm gonna install a little early warning lie detector in his subconscious. Charlie, from now on, every time you tell a lie . . . uh . . . you'll yodel!

Charlie

I'll yodel every time I tell a lie.

Sidemeat

Good. Okay, now I'm gonna count to three and you'll wake up. One, two, three, wake up!

Charlie

Huh? Say, what's going on around here? I tell ya I won't talk.

Sidemeat (aside to Riders)

Let's test my system . . . Charlie, is Slocum hiding out up in Thieves Canyon in a giant aerosol can?

Charlie

No, that's ridiculous. Yodel-ay-ee-tee.

Sidemeat

It works!

Charlie

What works?

Ranger Doug

Never mind. Just move on outta here and stay in front of us.

Charlie

Right . . . I'll stay way in front of you. Lookout, geezer!

Sidemeat

Nyah, huh?

Texas Bix

Suddenly, Charlie grabs Sidemeat and pushes him back into the Riders.

(Sfx: Sidemeat is pushed into the Riders. Charlie runs away.)

(Big Zeno Note: Grab yourself around the arms, grunt, and run in place.)

Woody Paul

Charlie's getting away!

Sidemeat

Let's get after that sidewinder!

                    Ranger Doug

Easy, Side, let him get a little bit of a head start.

                    Too Slim

But, Ranger Doug, he'll get away!

                    Ranger Doug

I don't think so, Too Slim. We know he's going somewhere in Thieves Canyon,
and if we just stay close to him he'll lead us right to Slocum.

                    Too Slim

Great thinking, Ranger Doug!

                    Ranger Doug

Thank you, Too Slim. It's that kinda thinking . . .

                    Sidemeat

We know, we know. Hadn't we better get after Charlie before he gets too much
of a head start on us?

                    Ranger Doug

Right, Side. C'mon boys, let's go!

(Joey: Hums fast and furious music.)

                    Texas Bix

Wasting no time, the Riders get to their horses and get after Charlie!

(Sfx: Horses galloping.)

                    Riders

Hyanh! Giddyup there!

(Sfx: Fade out galloping horses.)

                    Texas Bix

Ranger Doug's plan works to a T. And a short time later, from a narrow ridge in
the depths of Thieves Canyon, the Riders see Charlie gallop up to a giant aerosol
can and disappear inside it.

                    Woody Paul

There's the giant aerosol can!

                    Too Slim

Yeah, and there goes Charlie and . . . He's disappeared inside it! Gone!
Vanished! . . .

                    Ranger Doug

We get the picture, Too Slim.

                    Sidemeat

What are we waitin' for! Let's go get him!

Ranger Doug

Easy, Side, Slocum may have booby-trapped the area around that can. We'd better go slow and easy.

(Joey: Hums ominous, dramatic music.)

Texas Bix

As the Riders cautiously make their way across the canyon toward the giant aerosol can, inside the can, Charlie has entered a secret room and is reporting to Slocum.

Slocum

It's about time you got here, Charlie. What took you so long?

Charlie

I had a little run-in with Riders In The Sky.

Slocum

What? Did they follow you here?

Charlie

I dunno, boss. They could've. I had to make a pretty fast getaway.

Slocum

Actually, I hope they did follow you, Charlie. Let's check the ground radar here . . .

(Sfx: Three short beeps and one heehaw.)

Slocum

Look at those blips, Charlie! That means three men on horseback and one old geezer on a mule are closing in on us!

Charlie

That'd be them all right. What are we gonna do?

Slocum

Where's that Slim Whitman CD I sent you for.

Charlie

Here. But, how's that gonna help?

Slocum

I'm gonna use it to program my yodel-seeking hovering Sidewinder missile.

Charlie

What's it do?

Slocum

We fire this baby up in the sky, it's programmed to hover in the area until it hears a yodel, it will know what a yodel is from this Slim Whitman CD, then its steropulsar digital processor zeros in and . . .

Charlie

I know, boom! Right?

Slocum

Right. Now, I'll just load it in here . . . and there! It's ready to go! Push that red button there, Charlie.

Charlie

Right.

(Sfx: Button pushed.)

Slocum

There she goes!

(Sfx: Whoooooooooooooooooooooosh!)

(Big Zeno Note: Just say it—anything else is impractical.)

Charlie

Say, boss, what if Ranger Doug doesn't yodel?

Slocum

Charlie, how long you been in this game?

Charlie

Eh, since the beginning, boss.

Slocum

And how many times, when a melodrama's climax was approaching, has that cornball cowboy not yodeled?

Charlie

Uh, none.

Slocum

See what I mean?

Charlie

Oh . . . yeah. Say, looks like we got 'em this time, boss. Heh, heh, heh.

Slocum

We sure do, Charlie. Anybody yodels anywhere in this vicinity and that little Sidewinder hovering around out there in the sky will be up their royal wazoo at Mach three! Ha, ha, ha! By the way, Charlie, how much did that Slim Whitman CD cost me?

Charlie

Uh, twenty dollars, boss.

(Joey: Sting.)

Texas Bix

Meanwhile, Riders In The Sky have crested a small rise just across from Slocum's giant aerosol can when, suddenly, Ranger Doug calls a halt.

(Sfx: galloping horses.)

Ranger Doug

Whoa, Turbo!

(Sfx: Galloping stops.)

Too Slim

What is it, Ranger Doug?

Ranger Doug

There's a vapor trail flying around up there in the sky. Any idea what it is, Woody?

Woody Paul

Off hand, Ranger Doug, I'd say it's a Sidewinder missile cruising around in the ozone-depleted atmosphere at Mach three.

Sidemeat

Nyah, must be something Slocum's sending us.

Ranger Doug

Good thinking, Side. I think I'd better knock it out with a number three anti-aircraft yodel. Cover your ears, boys. Here goes!

Texas Bix

But as Ranger Doug opens his mouth to yodel, a small bug flies into his mouth and . . .

Ranger Doug

(Coughs and chokes.)

Too Slim

Oh, no. Is this the end of Riders In The Sky!

Woody Paul

I don't think so, Too Slim. Look, the missile is headed away from us and toward Slocum!

Texas Bix

Indeed it is, Woody Paul, and to find out why, one must only reflect back on a subliminal suggestion which Sidemeat implanted in Charlie's subconscious.

Charlie

(Short, bad yodel.)

Slocum

You mean there wasn't one cent in change from that twenty I gave you?

Charlie

Uh-uh. (Short, bad yodel.)

Slocum

A Slim Whitman CD costs twenty dollars?

Charlie

It sure does. (Short, bad yodel.)

Slocum

You wouldn't lie to me would you, Charlie?

Charlie

(Starts yodeling uncontrollably.)

Slocum

Charlie, are you yodeling? Stop that yodeling, you idiot! You're gonna get us killed! You swear there's no change?

(Sfx: Tremendous boom!)

(Big Zeno Note: Set off a firecracker in an iron kettle. If this is inappropriate, just say "Boom!" real loud.)

Texas Bix

I'm sure no further explanation is needed as to the measure of this poetic justice. A fact not lost on Riders In The Sky.

Ranger Doug

Well, that's that. The world is saved.

Too Slim

Yeah, but what about Tumbleweed Valley? We've got no ozone layer.

Woody Paul

Oh, don't worry about that, Too Slim. I'll get some volunteers from the Boy Scouts and the Girl Scouts and I'm sure I can have the ozone restored in no time.

Too Slim

Whew, that's a relief.

Ranger Doug

C'mon boys, let's head for home.

(Sfx: Horses ride off.)

(Joey: Closing theme.)

Texas Bix

Woody Paul was absolutely right, and within three days the ozone layer over Tumbleweed Valley was back to normal and once again there was peace in the valley. Within a few weeks a now-benevolent sun, along with plenty of cool spring showers, restored the grasses, wildflowers, and trees to their former beauty, and normal cattle roamed the range. Ducks could fly in peace over the valley and the ten-foot tall mutant prairie dogs were rounded up and shipped to Japan where they are the forthcoming stars of a major movie entitled *Teen-age Mutant Prairie Dogs Meet Godzilla*. That takes care of everything except for this brief scene from a luxury hotel suite in Palm Springs.

Marilyn

Dan, have you checked the answering machine lately?

Dan

No. I've really just been too busy to do it. I'd do it now, but I'm late for my tee-off time.

Marilyn

Don't worry about it, dear. We've never had an important message on it anyway. Have a good game!

Ranger Doug introduces Dry Wall Paul and Mamma prior to the release of *Livin' in a Mobile Home* for MCA Records. (Photo © David Skepner)

A HEARTFELT ♥ MESSAGE FROM DOCTOR WOODY CRACKCORN

Friends, believe it or not, you could walk out of your home on the range tomorrow morning and find your beloved herd engaged in compulsive over-grazing, excessive salt licking, or even, in the most severe cases, stampeding from reality. These are all symptoms of a psychological disturbance we at the **BOVINE PSYCHO-RESEARCH CENTER** call "Cow Dependency." When this happens your herd needs professional counseling help.

Now, I know that right now you're probably thinking, "Dr. Woody Crackcorn, if this happens to me I don't know what on earth I'll do! Why, with the price of beef being what it is and the continual rise of vegetarianism, I can't afford counseling for me and my better half, let alone my whole dang herd!"

Well, friends, don't panic. Doctor Woody Crackcorn wouldn't lead you out onto a limb and then saw it off. I have an economical solution to this problem for you. It is my new home study course entitled: **"COW-DEPENDENT NO MORE."** This comprehensive course comes to you on two 8-track tapes. Each tape deals with a different intra-herd dysfunction and they're priced at only $9.99 each. And, if you will act now, I'll also send you, absolutely free, a copy of the best-selling book about one-sided range relationships entitled: **"COWBOYS WHO HATE COWS, AND COWS WHO LOVE THEM"** by me, Doctor Woody Crackcorn.

TO ORDER CALL 1-900-NO-BEEFS.
DO IT TODAY! TOMORROW MAY BE TOO LATE!

Ranger Doug playing the
straight man for Woody
Paul. (Photo © 1991 David
Skepner)

Annie Laurie (Ranger
Doug's daughter) joins Too
Slim in the Armadillo Dance
in Austin, Texas, 1987.

At Fan Fair. (Photo © 1991
David Skepner)

Performing at the Cowboy
Poetry Gathering in Elko,
1990. (Photo © 1991 Sue
Rosoff)

Riders with Joey the
Cowpolka King, backstage
at the Grand Ole Opry.
(Photo © 1989 Don
Putnam)

Reading the comics between
takes at CBS studio,
summer 1991. (Photo ©
1991 Sue Rosoff)

Spots, CBS, 1991. (Photo ©
1991 Sue Rosoff)

*****ANYTIME IS PARTY TIME!!!!!

But with today's fast-paced lifestyles, who has time to roll scads of little sausages in pancakes, stuff dozens of mushrooms, or put Cheese Whiz on a gross of Ritz crackers?

BAG-O-BOILED EGGS

SAM & ELLA!
THAT'S WHO!

Yes, when you have SAM & ELLA'S CATERING bring the grub to your party or event, you have the makings of a truly memorial occasion! And we don't charge you an arm and a leg for it either! SAM & ELLA is cheap!!!

STACKS-O-MEAT

FROM A FAMILY OUTING—
TO A FAMILY REUNION!
FROM A LOVERS TETE-A-TETE
TO A VFW SMOKER!
YOU NEED SAM & ELLA!

BUCKET-O TATERS

"We supply unexpected culinary excitement! And the price you pay is unbelievable!"

WE CAN FEED A PARTY OF FIFTY FOR UNDER FORTY DOLLARS!

How can we be so cheap? Simple! We scrimp on quality and we don't waste money on expensive, unnecessary refrigeration!

We make up a year's supply of potato salad, coleslaw, boiled eggs, and barbecue in huge vats and fill your orders from them as they come in! We save a fortune in labor and electricity and we pass that savings along to you!

**SAM & ELLA'S
666 QUEASY STREET
Phone 1-900-SAM-ELLA**

"CALL US TODAY AND WE'LL GET YOU RIGHT AWAY!"

My Uncle Hank Peterson
and his old guitar, 1930s.

Strange Changes on the Range

AFTER NEARLY EVERY SHOW WE PLAY, a few buckaroos (and an occasional buckarette) will gather while we're signing autographs and begin remarking on my peculiar style of rhythm-guitar playing. As I am modest—with every reason to be modest!—about my playing, I generally hem and haw a bit, and someone usually pipes up with, "You ought to write a book so we can tell what you're doing!" (which would put them at least one step ahead of me!) Well, what I know about guitar playing would make for a mighty slim volume indeed, but it's good for at least a few pages in this one, in answer to all those requests.

First, a few moments of personal history: I first played my Uncle Hank's guitar when I was still in the single digits—he left it hanging on the wall in the little cabin he, his dad and his brother built on the Dead River Basin in the deep, deep piney woods of Northern Michigan. The times my family attempted to vacation on these far reaches of civilization, I'd generally try to play that old guitar. Turns out he and my mom used to sing the Lulu Bell and Scotty songs when they were young, which probably explains my genetic predisposition for harmony singing and guitar playing. Uncle Hank, by the way, doesn't play much any more—he hurt the fingers of his left hand some years ago, but is hale and healthy, full of enthusiasm and cheer, and is in his seventies, still an exercise and fitness fanatic, not unlike yours truly.

Ranger Doug picking a song,
CBS, 1991. (Photo © 1991
Sue Rosoff)

My brother Jim and I began playing in high school, and by college I'd decided on music as a career, although show business apparently didn't need me much at the time. I progressed from three- and four-chord playing to some more intricate work in Nashville, thanks to the enthusiasm and patience of a feller named Ron "King Chord" Hillis, who has since returned to his native Iowa. You can only learn so much from records, and having Ron, and later David Sebring, sit down and show me stuff was where I did the bulk of my learning. I'd have to say as far as recorded music, that all rhythm guitar playing fascinated me, and the playing of Henry Haynes (of Homer and Jethro) and Lloyd Perryman (of the Sons of the Pioneers) was particularly vivid and inspiring: Haynes' combination of grace, technique, and nonchalance, and Perryman's bouncy, swinging feel, that rocking western lope, stayed with me through the years.

So what I've done here is taken a song we commonly play, *Down The Trail to San Antone*, and broken it down to the individual chords—the primary chords and the passing chords—which I play as I chunk along "a chord every beat" (well, almost), as people often comment. It's a complex, difficult-looking, almost daunting style to see me play (I've seen it on tape, and durn, it *does* look impressive!) but for all that motion and seeming complexity, it is composed mostly of familiar chord patterns I use all the time in virtually every song we do. Fool with this song a while and you'll see that this is so. That's the reason I chose this song: it's challenging enough for a lot of players (and indeed it *is* hard to play at full speed), yet it is, because of the frequent repetition of the same patterns, easy enough for the neophyte rhythm king to play.

These are, of course, only the chords *I* play. Every good rhythm guitarist will have his own patterns and approaches, his choice of chord forms and voicings, fingerings that are easier for him (or her, of course) or more pleasant to the ear (or more intriguing) than these, just as you who are setting about to tackle this section will eventually have for yourself.

One final, and I'm sorry to say semi-discouraging word: if there can be said to be a "secret" to a "Ranger Doug Style," it is not in the left hand: any good rhythm guitar player knows these and many more chords. The unique quality of my sound is in the right hand. The peculiar lope I get, the distinctive feel and swing that is a part of the Riders' sound is the attack with the right hand, the combination of the muscular (but not brutal) "Sonny Liston strum" as my friend Jay Peterson called it, and the little hitch, or lope which propels (Woody and Slim might say confuses) the sound. That I can't diagram; each player just has to develop his own feel.

Good luck, happy landings, and don't give up: it wouldn't be the cowboy way!

A P.S. For Real Guitar Fanatics

Back when I was just Deputy Doug I used to do a lot of freelance writing, and I learned from doing several stories for *Guitar Player* and *Frets* that some people really care about what kind of guitar you play, so for you hard-core fanatics here's the info:

On stage I play a new 1991 Gibson L-5, with custom inlays designed and built by Jim Triggs and his staff at Gibson. It is a real honey, and I think in time its sound will grow and mature beautifully. It was built to replace the first custom L-5 they made for me (serial number 81308586), which disappeared on a flight from Nashville to Los Angeles in January of 1991. Some baggage handler has himself

Chords

Name of Chord

C

Finger to be Used

3 2 1

Nut
Fret 1
Fret 2
Fret 3
Fret 4
Fret 5

For those of you unfamiliar with these chord boxes, here is how they work:

Low ←→ High
Strings

a mighty nice guitar, but if you happen to see it, I'm offering a nice reward. It was built to replace the one guitar I really loved, a 1941 L-5 stolen from our bus in September of 1988. It was a sunburst cutaway, serial number 96514, and yes, there's a reward for that one, too, should you happen to run into it.

When I want a more open, ringing sound (as opposed to the woofing, driving sound of the L-5) I turn to a Gibson Advanced Jumbo, once again provided (but not custom built) by Jim Triggs at Gibson. Thanks, guys!

I have three I don't subject to road wear: a 1938 J-200, which just roars, a lovely little 1939 Martin 000-28 which I love to write songs on, and a 1949 D-28, which was the first good guitar I got on my own; I've been through a lot of instruments through the years, but never could part with that one. I use McCabe's medium-gauge strings on all but the 000-28. Okay, gang, technical corner is over, and we can go back to having fun now.

(Photo © 1991 Sue Rosoff)

NOTES

1. These first four chords are a little pattern I play all the time for chords out of the F position on the lower 4 strings; the next four are the similar pattern out of the C position on the middle 4 strings. These, of course, work all the way up the neck.

2. This is the way this chord is supposed to look according to my Mel Bay chord book, but to be honest with you—which *is* the cowboy way—I play this chord position by hooking my thumb over to catch the low string. Poor form but it works!

3. Sometimes I do just play one note to glide into the next chord. It's a) all you need, and b) the only way I know, take your pick.

4. This little "turnaround" is yet another hallmark of my imitable style.

Down the Trail to San Antone

Words by
Deuce Spriggins

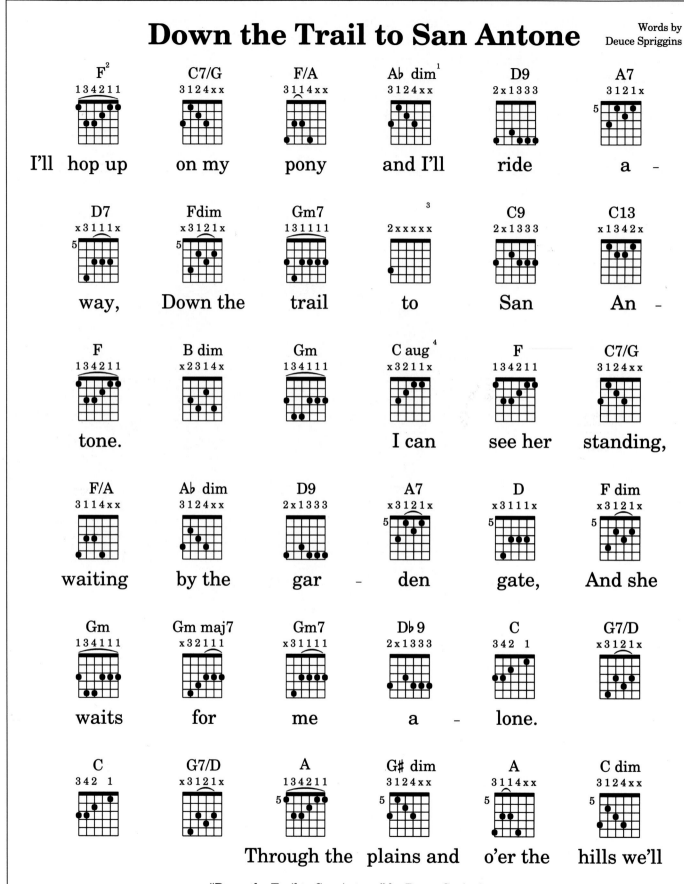

I'll hop up   on my   pony   and I'll   ride   a -

way,   Down the   trail   to   San   An -

tone.   I can   see her   standing,

waiting   by the   gar   -   den   gate,   And she

waits   for   me   a - lone.

Through the plains and o'er the   hills we'll

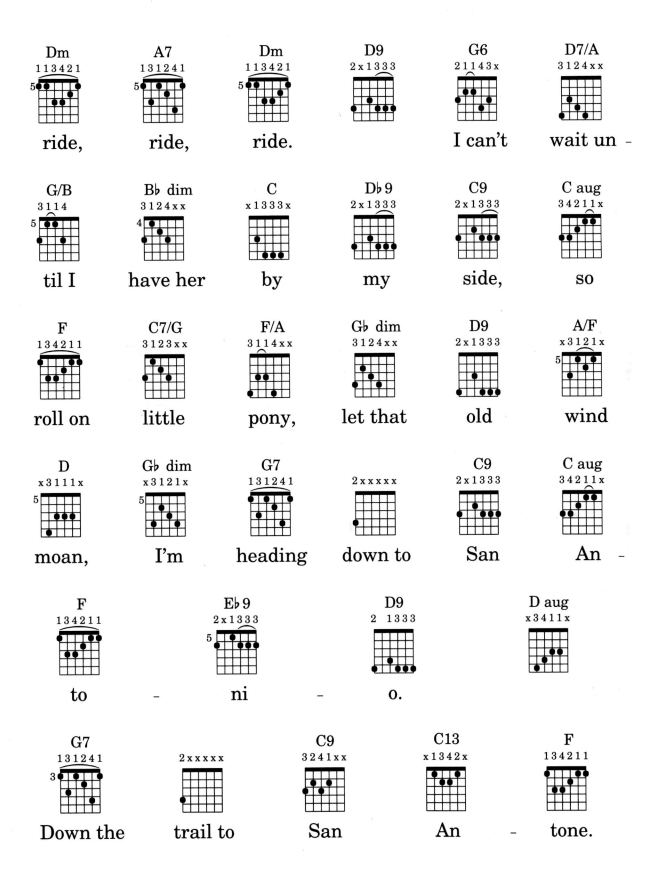

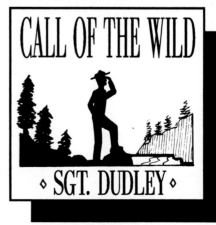
84

Prairie Lullaby

Words and Music by
Woody Paul

It's al - most time to leave you, It's been such fun be - ing with you; __ But the sun - set's col - ors now are fad - ing in the sky. _____ The twi - light's veil is fall - ing, __ Hear the night - bird __ soft - ly call - ing, __ As the eve - ning breez - es weave a prai - rie lul - la - by. _____ The sil - ver moon is sail - ing, The star - ry heav - ens deep. And all of na - ture's chil - dren are nes - tled down to sleep. So say your lit - tle prayers now, Close your eyes now, Go to sleep now, And to - mor - row we'll ride the trail to - geth - er a - gain.

Lonely Yukon Stars

Words and Music by
Douglas B. Green

Lone - ly Yu-kon stars gleam-ing high in the sky, Scat-tered care - less and lov - ing ___ by an art - ist on high. To their si - lent song the sigh-ing wind adds its part, A song that can on - ly be heard by the heart. North - ern lights that hang pale cur - tains of fire, Lead me to the one wait-ing warm by the fire. (fi - ery) Light - ly goes the moon on its mel-an - chol-y way, Guid - ing me home-ward as night be-comes day.

Yodel

Repeat Chorus

The Line Rider

Words and Music by
Douglas B. Green

There's a broken-down saddle on a peg on the wall,
Who knows how long it's hung there.
Like the hole in the soul of the lone buckaroo,
Too far gone for repair.
    Still his longing's as wide as the deep midnight sky,
    And as quiet as breaking of day.
So he saddles his pony and rides down the line;
It's the best he can do for today

Soon As The Roundup's Through

Words and Music by
Woody Paul

Clouds are roll-ing __ in __ a-cross the val-ley, __ A

night-bird sings __ a lone-ly mel-o - dy. __ The

cat-tle are __ a bed-din' on __ the banks of old __ Red Riv-er, __ I can

hear them __ soft-ly low - in' __ through the breeze.

Flames are dy - ing __ low __ now on the camp - fire, And

three months on __ the trail are near - ly gone. __ The

ech-o __ of __ a __ coy - ote's cry makes me give an emp - ty sigh, __ Don't

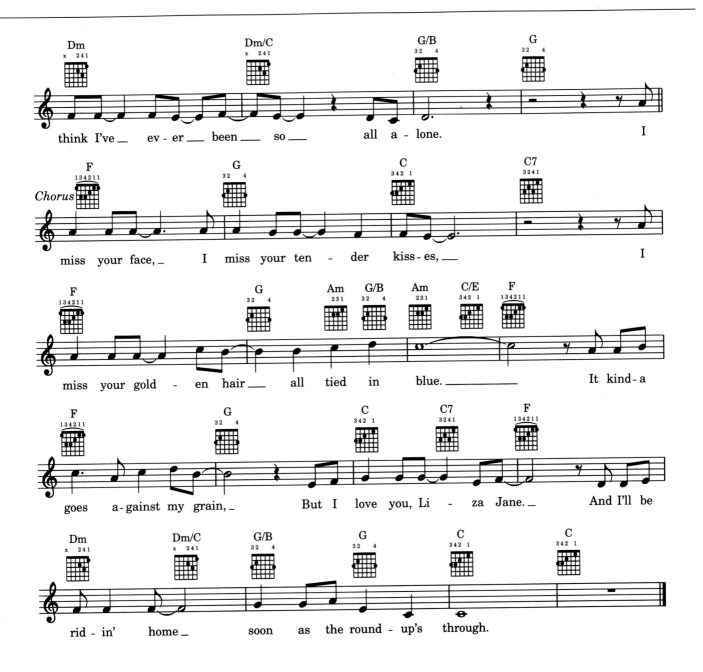

A year ago I saddled up my pony,
Said goodbye to you and all my friends.
I figure I might find myself way out on the trail somewhere,
But all I've found's another crook and bend.
I guess I was a crazy fool for leavin',
It felt like something I just had to do.
But I left the bigger part of this rovin' cowboy's heart,
It only beats when're I think of you.

Repeat Chorus

It kinda goes against my grain,
But I love you, Liza Jane,
And I'll be ridin' home soon as the roundup's through.

How Does He Yodel?

Words and Music by
Douglas B. Green

How does he yo - del? Yo - del a-dee ti. When does he yo - del? Yo - del a-dee ti.

Why does he yo - del? It sure beats me. Yo - del a-dee ti oh lay-dee ti. I

love to hear the cow-boys sing a hap-py yo-d'ling song, Some-thing makes me want to start just

yo-del-ing a-long. But way back in my ep - i - glot-tis, it al-ways ends up wrong,

Uh _____ Uh _____ Help, Rang-er Doug! How do we yo - del?

Yo - del a-dee doo. When do we yo - del? An-y time _ will do.

Why do we yo - del? I wish I knew. _ Boy, _ we _ do _ too. _

Cowboy Jubilee

Words by
Woody Paul and Fred LaBour

Music by
Woody Paul

Way out yon - der where the prai - rie winds blow, _ From the Ri - o Gran - de up to old I - da - ho, _ There's a sound comes wing - in' from o - ver the plains, _ It's the cow - boys a sing - in' the songs of the range. _ I want to be _ there when they ride in - to town. _ Can't get e - nough _ of that great west - ern sound. _ It's the best of the west, _ come a - long _ with me _ to the cow - boy ju - bi - lee.

Let the fiddle player blow a sweet melody,
Hear the cowboys answer with yodel-a-e-tee.
That bunkhouse bass never loses the beat,
That lopin' rhythm makes you want to kick up your feet.

I pick a prairie flower and I ask her to dance,
Once around the floor and it must be romance.
The prairie moon is shining for her and for me,
At the cowboy jubilee.

That's How the Yodel Was Born

Words and Music by
Douglas B. Green

When you hear a cow-boy yo-del-ing a song of o-pen range, Your heart leaps up to hear his stir-ring

tale. But did you ev-er won-der at the end of his re-frain, Why his voice leaps in a mourn-ful

wail? Well, the sto-ry as is told to me was hand-ed down through his-to-ry, Of a

sing-ing cow-boy brave e-nough to try To ride the mean-est old cay-use it

bucked him off right at the chute, Left him spin-ning way up in the sky. The

bron-co jumped up and the cow-boy came down, They met at the old sad-dle horn. It

made a deep im-pres-sion, you could say it changed his life, And that's how the yo-del was born.

Nevada

Words by
Woody Paul and Karen Ritter

Music by
Woody Paul

Ne - va - da, _____ sil - ver and sage - brush. Ne - va - da, _____ gam - blin' and gold - rush. _ Land of space and sun - shine. rocks and sky. Peo - ple who know her love Ne - va - da and here's why. _ Ne - va - da, _____ ranch - es and ghost - towns. _ Ne - va - da, _____ moun - tains with snow crowns. _ Ro - de - os and rail - roads, wild, rug - ged land. Deep night sky with stars like sil - ver sands. _

Nevada, Lake Meade and Tahoe.
Nevada, Vegas and Reno.
Land of dusty deserts, icy cold clear lakes.
Mustangs and juniper trees, and rattle snakes.

Nevada, silver and sage brush.
Nevada, gamblin' and gold rush.
The highest wildest country, the brightest, the best.
Nevada, the diamond of the west.

Ride With Me, Gringo

Words and Music by
Fred LaBour

He said, "We live high in the mountains,
With eagles and lions for brothers.
And we ride with brave señoritas,
With truest of hearts for our lovers,
We attack and we vanish,
Into the silvery light.
We're the bandits of sweet liberation,
Come join the army tonight.

Repeat Chorus

I awoke in the stillness this morning,
And Pancho Villa was gone.
I watched the sun on the mountains,
And I remembered the words to his song.
Now I give you my horse and my saddle;
Today I ride on a dream,
To a rendezvous in the mountains,
They're waiting for me by a stream.

Repeat Chorus

Last night I saw Pancho Villa.

Face: The Music

Words and Music by
Fred LaBour

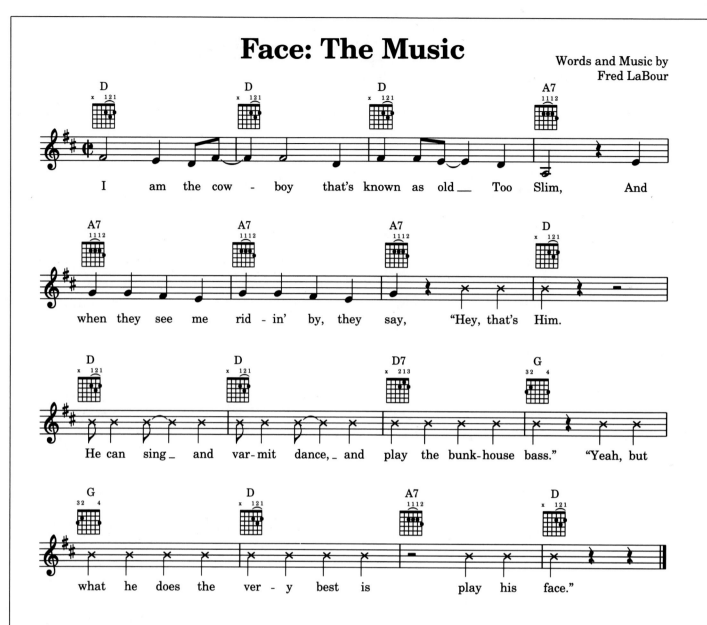

16 measures of face playing

It started many years ago when I was just a kid,
I'd get to feelin' cheeky and this is what I did;
I'd slap a little rhythm, I didn't feel like waitin',
And, after that I couldn't quit, it was so invigoratin'.

16 measures of face playing

So if you have a tune to play you really like a lot,
You don't need an instrument; just use the one you've got.
It's right between your hair and chin. Remember what I said,
You can play on any song if you just use your head.

32 measures of face playing

The Salting of the Slug

Words and Music by
Fred LaBour

freely

When first I came to Joel - ton, My for - tune there to find, I

met some jol - ly coun - try - men, On bar - be - cue we dined. The

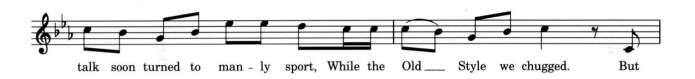

talk soon turned to man - ly sport, While the Old ___ Style we chugged. But

they said, "Lad, you had - n't lived, Till you have salt the slug."

They raised high their shakers full,
Of Morton's finest grain.
We crept out to the garden damp,
To there begin the game.
I watched each creature swell and pop,
Did thrill me to the core.
And every slug did learn that night,
That when it rains it pours.

So if you're e're in Joelton,
Quaffin' chilly brew.
And hearty lads and lassies fair,
Do salt a slug or two.
Pray join the sportin' company,
Forsaking sex or drugs.
God bless us jolly salters,
And take pity on the slugs.

LONGHORN LAND

THE WORLD'S ONLY AMUSEMENT PARK FOR BEEF ON THE HOOF!

Friends, our nation's beef is on the verge of extinction! Day after day of nothing more to do than cud chewing, grass grazing, and shoo fly shoo tail swatting is boring them to death!

THE RANGE ROLLER COASTER!

DOGIE BUMPER CARS!

MAKE PLANS TO BRING YOUR LISTLESS HERD TO LONGHORN LAND TODAY!

Longhorn Land is easily accessible to all major cattle trails.
Admission is only $9.99 a ton!
Give your herd a moo attitude!
To schedule a visit call 1-900-HERD-FUN!
(Feeder cattle rates available)

What can you do?
Round that herd up! and drive 'em down to the brand new wonder of the western world— Longhorn Land!

Longhorn Land is filled with marvelous sights and attractions to thrill the hearts of dogies of all ages!

MADAM DeBOSSY'S SPICY NEW ORLEANS HEIFER REVUE

MOO

WHERE'S THE BEEF!

WOO!

COWCESSION!

FLAVORED SALT LICKS

DEEP-FRIED CUD-ON-A-STICK

FUNNE FEED CAKES

THE SPECTACULAR 130-FT. WATER SLIDE

BRAND OF DEATH: THE ROLLING R BAR X FLYING D LUCKY 7 TUMBLING T LAZY B WALKING T RANCH

100

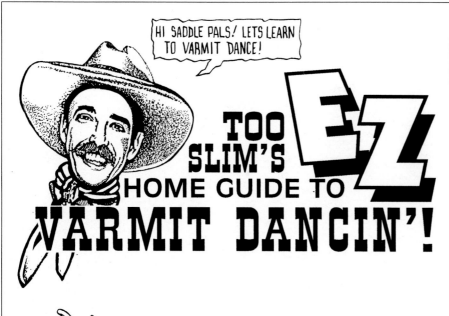

HI SADDLE PALS! LETS LEARN TO VARMIT DANCE!

TOO SLIM'S EZ HOME GUIDE TO VARMIT DANCIN'!

Welcome buckaroos and bucka-rettes, to my EZ Home Guide to Varmit Dancin'! If you'll spend just 15 minutes with me right now, I'll help you master this truly foolish fad in the privacy of your own home!

Okay, take a few minutes to loosen up and then let's get started!

Okay, let's go! First, put on a tape of silly fiddle music—good! Now just follow the charts below and let's varmit dance!

THE RABBIT DANCE

All varmit dancing starts with The Rabbit Dance. To begin with, bend over, keeping your feet flat on the floor and put the palms of your hands flat on the floor . . . that's it! Keep your fanny high in the air and Hop! Hop! Hop! That's great! Now say: "I was born to Rabbit Dance!"

Okay, you're ready for some advanced varmit dancin' now! Here's one I picked up while hanging around in South America.

THE THREE-TOED SLOTH DANCE

First, look around the room and locate a low-hanging timber, a railing of some kind, or maybe just a sturdy chair or sofa arm . . . got it? All right! Run to it, throw a leg over it, grasp it in both hands; now throw the other leg over it and hang on. Now what-ever you do, don't move . . . you're doing The Three-Toed Sloth Dance! (Look at those smooth moves!)

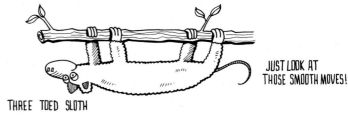

THREE TOED SLOTH

JUST LOOK AT THOSE SMOOTH MOVES!

All right, take a moment to catch your breath and then let's move on to the most famous varmit dance of all!

THE ARMADILLO DANCE

Note: The governor of Kansas considers this dance to be too disgusting to be performed in polite society, and it is banned in that state pursuant to executive order no. 0358769123.

Get down on your hands and knees, crawl three feet and stop. Now, look to the left and look to the right. Nothing is coming, so crawl on two more feet and . . . oh no, you didn't see that truck! On, no! It got you! Fall on the floor, roll over flat on your back and lie there. You're doing The Armadillo!

That's it! You can Varmit Dance!

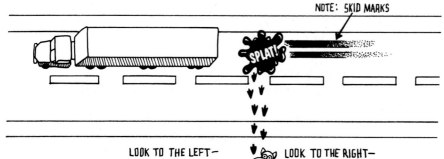

NOTE: SKID MARKS

LOOK TO THE LEFT— NOTHING COMING THIS WAY...

LOOK TO THE RIGHT— NOTHING COMING THAT WAY...

ARMADILLO

Ranger Doug.
(Photo © 1991 Sue Rosoff)

The picture of grace
and confidence.
(Photo © 1986 Alan
L. Mayor)

Woody Paul. (Photo
© 1992 Don Putnam)

(Photo © 1991 Sue Rosoff)

Too Slim as Trapper in Baxter Black's video *The Spur*, 1990. (Photo © 1991 Sue Rosoff)

(Photo © 1991 Sue Rosoff)

(Photo © 1992 Don Putnam)

109

THE MAMMOTH MIRACLE HOT SPRINGS COW WASH!

HERE'S THE MODERN ANSWER TO DIRTY, DINGY, DISCONTENTED HERDS!

THIS AMAZING, FULLY AUTOMATED COW WASH FEATURES THE LATEST IN BOVINE HYGIENIC TECHNOLOGY!

Patented 360° high-pressure detergent hoops. These powerful water jets reach all those messy, **hard-to-reach places** and blast the grime out.

Next, our **unique brisket brushes** churn thick, cleansing suds all over the hide.

Then **humane** foam-covered wringers remove excess moisture.

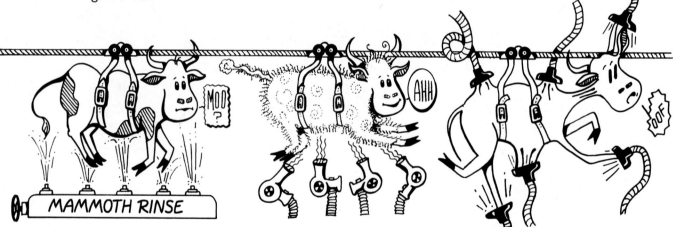

This is followed by a final rinse, which adds a liberal dose of **industrial-strength** Downy.

Next, gentle blow dryers fluff them up to a softness you won't soon forget and they virtually **float to the next stop . . .**

where high-powered vacuum cleaners **remove build-up from ears, rears, and everywhere in between!**

So head 'em up, move 'em out and drive 'em through the Mammoth Miracle Hot Springs Cow Wash. It's reasonably priced at only $9.99 a ton!

Mammoth Miracle Hot Springs Cow Washes are an indispensable feature at most modern conestoga stops across the West!

(Photo © 1991 Sue Rosoff)

(Photo © 1991 Sue Rosoff)